REVIVAL

Including the Prophetic Vision of Jean Darnall

Other books by the same author:

Reflections on the Baptism in the Holy Spirit
Reflections on the Gifts of the Spirit
Reflections on a Song of Love (1 Cor 13)
A Trumpet Call to Women
The Clash of Tongues: With Glimpses of Revival
Consider Him (Twelve Qualities of Christ)
Battle for the Body
The Incomparable Christ
Gospel Vignettes
Reflections from Abraham
Reflections from Moses: With the Testimony of Dan McVicar
Christ the Deliverer
Christian Fundamentals
Reflections from David
Pioneers of the Spiritual Way
Revival: Personal Encounters
Revival: Living in the Realities

REVIVAL

*Including the Prophetic Vision
of Jean Darnall*

HUGH B. BLACK

NEW DAWN BOOKS
GREENOCK, SCOTLAND

First published 1993 by
NEW DAWN BOOKS
27 Denholm Street, Greenock PA16 8RH, Scotland

ISBN 1 870944 15 1

Unless otherwise stated, biblical references
in Part One are to the Revised Version.

Production and Printing in England for
NEW DAWN BOOKS
27 Denholm Street, Greenock PA16 8RH, Scotland by
Nuprint Ltd, Station Road, Harpenden, Herts AL5 4SE.

*To the memory
of saints of old who have
pioneered the way of revival*

CONTENTS

ACKNOWLEDGEMENTS

I am grateful to my wife Isobel and to Miss Pauline Anderson, Mr Alistair Duff and Miss Jennifer Jack for proof-reading and helpful contributions. My daughter Alison processed and helped to edit the material from tape-recordings through various drafts.

In particular I wish to thank Mrs Jean Darnall for allowing me to incorporate in this book the telling of her vision and the sermon she preached in Glasgow City Halls in June 1987.

My thanks are also due to the authors and publishers whose works have been quoted. Detailed acknowledgement is made in the notes.

FOREWORD

Some ask, 'What can be done?' Others, more pressingly, urge, 'Something must be done.' We live in increasingly troubled times. With mounting concern over world events men are searching everywhere for an answer to their problems.

Jean Darnall received a vision, an exciting vision, a revelation of the intention of God towards our nation: and it is in fact being outworked today. Therein lies the answer to man's need. There is only one source of healing and only one means whereby it may come — by divine intervention and the ushering in of revival.

In the following pages the reader will find much encouragement. God, having moved in the past — and in the very recent past — will certainly do so again.

For some time many of us have known a considerable unease at the turn of events with the accompanying moral declension. We have also been aware that there is a key which unlocks the door into another dimension, the key of prevailing prayer, and yet so few are willing to use it. However, if we care, we can no longer evade the challenge. Let complacency give way to compassion and urgent intercession until we receive the answer — the fire of God in the church.

May it be that, as we read these pages, we shall be inspired to present ourselves as willing instruments in the day of His power, and to lay hold upon God until revival comes.

Jessie S. Wallace

EXPLANATORY NOTE

In this book there is an attempt to take readers in spirit into the meetings in which the teaching now produced in written form was first presented. This accounts for the inclusion of prayers, exhortations, and other linking material. (Initials enclosed in square brackets after the heading of such items denote the individual, other than the author, through whom some of this material came). Obviously a listening audience was first addressed — but now the material is adapted to suit a reading audience also.

A similar approach was taken in two of my latest books, *Christian Fundamentals* and *Pioneers of the Spiritual Way*, and they seem to have been happily received. I trust that this too will be generally approved.

INTRODUCTION

Through most of a lifetime I have been interested in revival. It was not a theme which was emphasized in the group in which I had my earliest spiritual instruction, but I became aware of it through my own early reading about Charles G. Finney and the early Methodists. The Welsh revival of 1904 I found fascinating, and the writings of Norman Grubb led me into a deepening understanding of underlying principles.

About thirty years ago a lady much used of God, a real prophetess, spoke to me of God's revelation to her of coming days in Scotland. She had secured a book on the Scottish Covenanters which greatly kindled her spirit. She read of the hills of Scotland stained with the blood of the martyrs and her own age as one with little interest in religion. Something seemed to happen within her. A cry was born and a great desire for a quickening. I remember she said that God gave her a scripture related to Elijah's servant seeing a cloud 'the size of a man's hand'. It was the sign of the coming deluge of rain. God caused her to look and she too saw a cloud the size of a man's hand and had assurance that the floodtides would come. This vision was never forgotten and the theme of revival was kept constantly before our fellowship.

In recent years there has been an increasing conviction amongst many people that revival is coming nearer in Scotland. I have had the privilege of knowing people, some of them intimately, who have been deeply involved in it in the past, and I now feel the time has come to write about it and, I hope, focus attention as one means of promoting it.

Jean Darnall, a well-known and much-loved leader of

the charismatic renewal in Britain, has graciously given me permission to include in my book her vision of revival which she saw starting in the north of Scotland and moving south through England and across the Channel to Europe. Her vision contains remarkable and to me quite unexpected features. It has deeply affected many audiences with whom she has already shared it. The narration of her vision and the sermon she preached in Glasgow, June 1987, form Part 2 of the book.

This book is the first of a trilogy planned on the subject of revival. In it I do not attempt to survey all the major revivals of the last two centuries. Rather I have been selective, concentrating on some of those which have most affected me personally and about which I have some detailed knowledge. I use them to illustrate recurring patterns and to emphasize enduring principles of revival. I have felt it wise to approach the subject in this way to help to prepare people for the hour when God visits our land in power again.

The sequel, *Revival: Personal Encounters*, offers personal reminiscences related to revival. These have proved of interest to audiences over the years and will perchance contribute to a quickened awareness of what God purposes to do in this our day.

The third of the trilogy is *Revival: Living in the Realities*. This deals with issues of spiritual concern to those who have been revived.

PART ONE

PAST REVIVALS
Principles and Practices

*B*ehold, I send my messenger, and he shall prepare the way before me: and the Lord, whom ye seek, shall suddenly come to his temple; and the messenger of the covenant, whom ye delight in, behold, he cometh, saith the LORD of hosts. But who may abide the day of his coming? and who shall stand when he appeareth? for he is like a refiner's fire, and like fullers' soap: And he shall sit as a refiner and purifier of silver, and he shall purify the sons of Levi, and purge them as gold and silver; and they shall offer unto the LORD offerings in righteousness.... And I will come near to you to judgement; and I will be a swift witness against the sorcerers, and against the adulterers, and against false swearers; and against those that oppress the hireling in his wages, the widow, and the fatherless, and that turn aside the stranger from his right, and fear not me, saith the LORD of hosts (Mal 3:1–5).

For, behold, the day cometh, it burneth as a furnace; and all the proud, and all that work wickedness, shall be stubble: and the day that cometh shall burn them up, saith the LORD of hosts, that it shall leave them neither root nor branch. But unto you that fear my name shall the sun of righteousness arise with healing in his wings; and ye shall go forth, and gambol as calves of the stall. And ye shall tread down the wicked; for they shall be ashes under the soles of your feet in the day that I do make, saith the LORD of hosts (Mal 4:1–3).

Break up your fallow ground: for it is time to seek the LORD, till he come and rain righteousness upon you (Hos 10:12).

1 | Breaking up the Fallow Ground

PRAYER:[1] *Lord, we pray for an increase in power, for the moving of Thy Spirit. We need Thee, O God; we feel the need of Thee very particularly. That wicked one opposes that which Thou dost desire to speak in the ears of men, and we realize our need, our dependency. We pray that we shall stand out of the way, so that there shall come a wave of the Holy Spirit, an emanation of power, a wave of conviction. Lord, beyond the natural, beyond the human, beyond mere words let there be power and let there be glory, let there be majesty and let there be awe, we pray Thee, in the name Lord Jesus Christ and for His sake. Amen.*

Revival Defined

I do not remember a time in my life, which comprises a fair part of this century, when there has been amongst Christians generally such a consciousness that revival is coming, such a widespread conviction and sense that God will visit His people in this way.

You may say, 'That is very good and very hopeful.' But if I begin to ask people what they expect to happen, what they understand by the coming of revival, you might really be quite shocked at the answers, because there is not, in fact, generally a clear-cut knowledge of what revival is, how it comes, and what the consequences of it are. There is a vague idea that it is a time of soul-winning,

19

a time of blessing, a time when the church is happy and joyous and the songs of Zion are on the lips of the saints.

Let me tell you: revival is a very fearful thing. It is a soul-shattering thing. It is a community-moving thing. It is wonderful, it is glorious, but it is awesome and very terrible. It is not to be prayed for lightly, and you must have no expectation of entering into it lightly. It can change your whole life; it can change you radically at depths of which you have no present knowledge, and you will never be the same again.

The Coming of Conviction

I remember the definition that the late Duncan Campbell gave. He said in effect, 'Revival is neither more nor less than the impact of the personality of Jesus Christ upon a church or upon a community or upon an individual life.' It is the impact of the personality of Christ. Our God is a consuming fire, and when revival draws near to a community, there is a coming of fire. There is a strange, awesome sensation. There is conviction of sin, deep, terrible and inescapable: not a matter of the sins that *you* particularly choose to think about, choose to examine; but the sins that are brought before you by the power of the Holy Spirit. You cannot alter the revelation, you cannot change it by a hairbreadth. It is the word and the revelation of the living God, and you must accept the divine verdict on your condition and on the sin that is in your life. Awful, fearful: things that you have been hiding for a lifetime come under the strong searching glare of the Son of God, and God's judgment is absolute. And you know, in that hour of revelation when the power of it grips a church, a community, or an individual (and it always comes down to individuals), you suddenly lose all consciousness of the sins of other people. You are concerned only with your own sin and shortcoming, nothing else. The ground is very level at Calvary, and every man bears his own burden and endures his own conviction in the day of the Lord, when His power is revealed. God draws near, and there comes the burning fire and conviction of sin.

Confession

Follow the normal course through, and you will find that the conviction becomes so intense that there are people who are compelled just to pour out their condition in confession, and sometimes publicly. I remember Miss Taylor[2] used to say, 'Get right with God now while you can do so privately, because if you don't and you are caught out in the day of God's power, what could have been dealt with privately will come bursting out publicly, for you will be unable to stand the pressure of the revelation of God.' In revival sin is brought to the surface. People can't hold it, can't stand it, are desperate to be done with it, to be clean, to be clear, under the strong pressures of God.

I remember Mr Campbell saying that when revival broke out from time to time in Lewis it was like the exploding of a bomb. Suddenly there was no more need for preaching, and he would sit down. Something burst in the atmosphere, and all over the congregation people were affected, some lying prostrate, some in one position, some in another. The Holy Spirit was dealing with them one by one. You could find that before one man's feet hell was opening; you could find that another was brought under terrible conviction for something wrong that he had to put right before he could get through to God. You would find that there would be conviction about relationships, attitudes, and, across the board, sin in general. God would call for immediate surrender, immediate obedience, immediate breaking. And after God broke men, deeply broke them, there would come the flood of salvation: converts would be born not of man but of God; born in depth, born in power, born into glory.

The Coming of Glory

Men and women saved in that kind of situation seldom ever backslide. A man who has seen hell and known that his soul has been dangled over the flaming fire is not apt to backslide. It is too real, too awesome, too awful. They would find the Lord, and then the glory would fall. And the place would become alive with God, the atmosphere electric. The movement would spread out and out beyond the congregation affected until in Lewis many found the Son of God. Along these lines comes revival.

How It Begins

Now you may say, 'How does it begin?' Normally it begins in the heart of one individual, or in the hearts of a small group of individuals; and it does not begin with God complimenting men on their holiness. It frequently begins with the best people in a church or in a community. God often puts His hand on the most saintly, and they are bowed down with the burden of God. In so far as there is anything to put right in their lives, that is first dealt with. And then the burden of prayer and of intercession comes upon them. Gradually others of like mind are joined to them, and they bear the burden and go through with God. They receive the promises and they believe the promises. They become channels for the Holy Spirit. The burden of revival comes upon their hearts. Gradually the movement spreads out further.

Lewis Recalled

My memory goes to Lewis and what I know of the beginning of revival in the parish of Barvas. A small group of praying people were meeting night by night to pray for revival. In a remarkable way Mr Campbell had found himself on the Island to take a series of meetings.³ These had commenced, but nothing in particular had happened on the first night. Then he was invited to join an all-night prayer meeting, which he did, and he said that some time near dawn (I seem to recollect) there came a knowledge that they had got through to God. *Who shall ascend into the hill of the LORD? And who shall stand in his holy place? He that hath clean hands, and a pure heart* (Ps 24:3−4). There was a being right with God, and they knew they were through to the throne. An absolute faith that revival would come was born.

On the following night revival broke out. As the people were beginning to go from the church, a young man fell prostrate and prayed fervently. He seemed to go out of the body, and power fell across those of the congregation who were still in the church and also on those who were outside amongst the boulders of the churchyard. God began to revive His people. What happens in such an hour is beyond our human understanding. It changes the lives of men and communities, and it can happen in a few minutes of time. But note, there was a going through to God; there were people prepared for the hour of God's power. Normally, as I have said, it begins with a few people having the burden of intercession, the burden of prayer, sharing as it were in the very heart of God.

Misunderstandings about Revival

Revival is a much misused word. It is a word that you very seldom read anywhere in the Bible. It is not a concept that you meet much, if at all, in the New Testament. And for that there is a very good and understandable reason. Revival means the bringing to life again of that which has died or is dying. And the New Testament does not regard such a condition as normal. It does not in any way condone a Christian's being other than in a state of livingness, a state of life. It is totally wrong to be backslidden in any measure, in any sense. And the New Testament views Christians as men and women who are following Christ, who are going on with God. When you use the word revival, you are assuming a condition of death into which life is to come again. As a result, you do not read of revival in the Bible in the way that we tend to use the term. Indeed, we do not tend to use it accurately as I have defined it here. You will find one foolish kind of use: 'We're going to have revival services,' as though we could turn on revival. Now that is a nonsense. You cannot turn on revival. But even so, when we realize it is a bringing to life again of that which is dead, it is obvious that this is not quite what we usually mean by the word revival. Rather we associate the word with much of the power and the phenomena that are witnessed in revival time. And of course much of that is amongst people who are being drawn in, rather than amongst people being revived.

Stages of Development

The normal stages of development are these: concern in the hearts of an individual or of a small group, a cleansing within their hearts of sin and the coming upon them of a very real burden of prayer and intercession, a growing conviction and concern amongst others, and the bursting out of the floods of life, sometimes triggered by the preaching of an anointed channel and sometimes spontaneously, a flooding of divine life into and beyond the immediate community, right out to the unsaved people in an area or in a whole country.

A Passing Generation

These are classic stages in the moving of revival. Now there are very few people in our own land today who have ever been involved in revival, or witnessed it, or even sensed the 'spirit of revival', if I might use that phrase. There are some, although a fast-diminishing number, of the older people in Lewis who of course do remember it. There are, I would imagine, very few people who remember anything of the Welsh revival; few of these will be still alive. In fact we are in an age in Britain where living memory of revival has almost completely gone. I was myself with Duncan Campbell in the later stages of his visiting Lewis; I chauffeured him to the first nights of his campaign in Gravir. But the revival by that time had largely passed, and it did not break out when I was there. My only personal experience of revival was at a school camp to which I refer in a forthcoming book. I will not go into detail now, but I can tell you that I was moved to the depths of my being. It was an awesome, fearful, wonderful time.

Finney

I want to take this subject in measured stages, not to present too much material undiluted, and I first turn to some of the earliest revivals of which I had very much knowledge — those in America associated with Charles G. Finney, and the revival in Britain associated with the Wesley brothers and Whitefield.

I want to look into the revival in America very briefly, but bring some of the salient points before you. I often think of Finney as a high priest or apostle of revival, if I may use such terms. I associate revival more with Finney than I do with any person who has lived between Paul's day and our own. He gave very vital, very critical teaching on revival. He seems to have come under a terrible burden to commit to writing teaching on the subject. Not until he had done so did the burden lift. I believe that between his day and ours he has had an effect, direct or indirect, on many of the revivals that have broken out in various parts of the world. The connections that go back to Charles G. Finney are amazing.

I was first introduced to Finney (if I may put it that way) when I was a comparatively young man, a boy almost. And I shall never forget what I read about him then. I do not know how the literature had come into my hand, but I remember it so clearly. Within twenty-four hours of his salvation, he said,

> I received a mighty baptism of the Holy Ghost. Without any expectation of it, without ever having the thought in my mind that there was any such thing for me, without any recollection that I had ever heard the thing mentioned by any person in the world, the Holy Spirit descended upon me in a manner that seemed to go through me, body and soul. I could feel the impression, like a wave of electricity, going through and through me. Indeed it seemed to come in waves and waves of liquid love, for I could not express it in any other way. It seemed like the very breath of God. I can recollect distinctly that it seemed to fan me, like immense wings.
>
> No words can express the wonderful love that was shed abroad in my heart. I wept aloud with joy and love; and I know not but I should say, I literally bellowed out the unutterable gushings of my heart.[4]

And Finney was baptized in the Holy Spirit, speaking in tongues — although we do not learn that from this excerpt.[5] He was baptized in the Spirit, and there came over him a power to promote revival. And he moved under that power. People were strangely affected by his words, pierced to the heart, turning to God. He said there were times when the power faded, and he had to go alone and fast and pray until it came back upon him; but he was not prepared to live without that power. Do you know that almost everywhere Finney went, revival went? When Finney began to preach, there were approximately six hundred thousand Christians in the United States of America. When he was finished, there were six million, for many of whom he had been God's instrument. On one occasion, in a matter of weeks, hundreds of thousands were born again. And it has been said that where ten of Moody's converts backslid, only one of Finney's did so. His standards were extreme, his demands were awful, as a soul came to find Christ. Unless there was absolute submission to Christ without reservation, he held out no hope of salvation to the enquirer. He would go into an area, and if a church, for example, did not obey his teaching he would leave them. He refused to waste time; he might give about three days to obey what he considered to be the teaching of God on revival, and either they would break, or he would leave.

Breaking the Ground

In his writings he gives particular instruction about the theme of revival. In line with the text, *Break up your fallow ground*, he taught that a farmer does not sow seed for fun; he sows seed to reap a harvest. Nor does he go out and sow seed on unbroken soil, for then he would reap no harvest. He first takes the plough and he drives that plough through the soil, breaking the sods, turning over the fallow ground. He thoroughly breaks up the ground. The farmer will plough his land, and sometimes if it is necessary he will cross-plough it so that it is thoroughly broken up. The farmer, Finney said, sows in faith, expecting to reap a harvest. And year after year after year, he reaps a harvest. There are laws in nature that cause the reaping of the harvest to follow the sowing of the seed, laws that operate from year to year and from century to century.

Now, he said, the farmer has a right to expect a harvest when he breaks up his fallow ground and sows the appropriate seed at the appropriate time. In the same way, you can expect to have a spiritual harvest when you break up the fallow ground of your hearts and receive the good seed from God and let it take root.[6] In our countryside, the plough goes in, the grain is sown, the harrows come over to put the soil back on top of the grain, the roller comes on top of that so that in the time of reaping there will be a good foundation, and our farmers expect and regularly reap their harvests.[7]

We turn to the spiritual. Finney's message was: 'Break up your fallow ground. Let the plough of the Word of God enter into your hearts. Let the ploughshare cut deep into your hearts.'

You may say, 'Well, how do you do that? How does that happen?'

Sins of Commission and Omission

The word of God brings that into being. Finney brought the word to bear on the lives of his enquirers. He helped in uncovering the sin that made the ground hard and unable to receive the good seed in that condition. To do this, he listed a number of sins that are normal and common amongst the unrevived. He said, take paper and write them down. Make a list against each where you are guilty. When you have gone through the list, go through it again and you will find that one sin brings another to your memory. Write them all down. Write them down, until you are thoroughly broken up as your iniquity is revealed to you. Here are the headings of the sins of commission that he listed, and you can ask yourself if you are guilty:

  Worldly mindedness
  Pride
  Envy
  Censoriousness
  Slander
  Levity

Lying
Cheating
Hypocrisy
Robbing God
Bad temper
Hindering others from being useful.[8]

I remember when I first met that list — oh, was I shattered! But this was not all. Besides the sins of commission, Finney listed the sins of omission:

Ingratitude
Want of love to God
Neglect of the Bible
Unbelief
Neglect of prayer
Neglect of the means of grace
The manner in which you have performed those duties
Want of love for the souls of your fellow-men
Want of care for the heathen
Neglect of family duties
Neglect of social duties
Neglect of watchfulness over your own life
Neglect to watch over your brethren
Neglect of self-denial.[9]

Results of Revival

Such an approach doesn't leave very much room for turning around. Finney and his teaching went like fire through America, although mightily opposed by many Christian people. The fire caught and the fire blazed and transformed men in an exceedingly wicked America (it was in a fearful condition when Finney began: fearful in the depth of its sin). Much of a nation was affected.[10] Blessed be the name of the Lord.

Do you still want revival, remembering that it starts

with you, it starts with me? Can we say, 'Blessed be the name of the Lord'?

> PRAYER: *Lord, help us to prepare ourselves for what many of us have a conviction that You are going to do in Scotland. You are going to send a burning, powerful revival. Lord, we don't expect it to be on the lines of any revival that has ever been, for each revival has its own dimension, its own peculiar characteristics. Lord, we would not have people fall into legalism, and we realize that in trying to dig up sin there can be a human side which is not always healthy. It is often essential for those who are careless and heedless to introspect deeply. But, O God, we cannot be rid of sin merely by finding what we have done and trying to repent of it; the forgiveness of sin comes from Yourself, by the application of the blood of Christ. And, Lord, we would not usurp any of Your functions. Nor would we have people go into any kind of wrong bondage. But we do pray that there shall be a probing of us every one to bring us to the light, that we may be judged, not by Finney's list, or by our own list, but by the Spirit of God. It is He who convicts of sin and leads into all truth. We ask it in Christ's name. And we ask now, Lord, that You will open up to us some of the consequences of being revived, and something of the depth of the life into which You would bring Your people. We ask it in the name Lord Jesus Christ and for His sake. Amen.*

Notes

1 The address recorded in this chapter was preceded by an exhortation and prayer by Miss Mary Black which may be of interest to readers. See Appendix 1.
2 For Miss Taylor's story, see the author's *A Trumpet Call to Women* (New Dawn Books, 1988), Part 2.
3 See chap. 6 below.
4 *Charles G. Finney: An Autobiography* (Fleming H. Revell

Company, undated repr. of 1876 edition entitled *Memoirs of Charles G. Finney*), p. 20.

[5] Although it is not explicitly stated in the passage quoted above that Finney spoke in tongues, the evidence exists elsewhere: see Hugh B. Black, *The Clash of Tongues: with Glimpses of Revival* (New Dawn Books, 1988), Appendix 7.

[6] In this matter Finney undoubtedly puts great emphasis on human responsibility and the need for man to take action in relation to revival. He has been criticized for not sufficiently emphasizing the divine element — perhaps sometimes unfairly. It has also been suggested that his success was related to the fact that he operated in a season of revival, which some would maintain came in God's sovereign will and in His time — and that the teachings Finney gave would not necessarily work at all times and places.

In brief, Finney taught that we can have revival when we like. All we have to do is meet God's conditions. Critics maintain that we cannot bring revival by following a blueprint. Only God can bring it.

In my view we should fulfil our part, and we can safely leave God's part with Him. There are undoubtedly two sides to the matter, as there are in so many spiritual issues, for example salvation itself — divine action and human response. Where revival is concerned, Finney would maintain that God has already acted in giving clear instructions as to how men ought to act, and when we obey these we can confidently expect Him to meet us with revival outpouring.

In how far a God-called instrument (see chap. 2 below) and 'seasons of refreshing' affected the outcome of Finney's ministry is intriguing. We should certainly not discard our responsibilities too lightly and sit passively waiting on revival coming upon us. We have a part to play. Many critics of Finney, it must be admitted, would agree that this is so — but the question is, how great a part. Some feel that Finney went too far in his views.

Colin Whittaker writes: 'Finney clearly swung the pendulum too far in his reaction against the fatalism that had well nigh paralysed his denomination at that time. The great awakenings of 1739; 1857–59; 1904–5; and the like, were not planned, programmed or promoted. "It must therefore be concluded," says Edwin Orr, "that Finney's principles applied to local efforts of renewal or evangelism rather than to widespread movements of the Holy Spirit.'' See Colin Whittaker, *Great Revivals* (Collins: Marshall Pickering, 1990; first published by Marshall Pickering, 1984), pp. 168–169.

7 See Charles G. Finney, *Revival Lectures*, also entitled *Revivals of Religion* (Fleming H. Revell Company, n.d.), pp. 5–6, 29–30.

8 Finney discusses each of these sins of commission in *Revival Lectures*, pp. 42–5.

9 See ibid., pp. 38–42.

10 It should be remembered, of course, that there were powerful revivals in America before Finney's day. Those associated with Jonathan Edwards and George Whitefield were remarkable. But it remains true that godlessness was rife and much of the established church was deeply opposed to the movement of God under Finney.

2 | MORE ABOUT FINNEY

PRAYER AND EXHORTATION [MB]: *The vision is glorious; it is for an appointed time: the vision of the oncoming wave of the glory of God, the power of revival in this our land. Grip the hearts of Your own people, Lord, with revival power; grip the hearts of Your own with the spirit of prayer and intercession for the healing of our land. Praise fills our hearts. Oh, lift up your eyes and see the vision of the oncoming wave of glory.*

O God our heavenly Father, we joy in the glorious truth of these words, that Your coming is as 'the morning on the wave', and there is a glory coming toward us as we lift our eyes to that far horizon. We see the glory of the second coming of the Lord Jesus Christ, and know that this hour is part of the preparation of the church of Christ for that glorious advent. We would be numbered amongst the lovers of Christ whose hearts are fixed and cannot be moved, whose whole beings are riveted to the glory of that radiant Christ.

O God, bring the sense of the Lord Jesus and the imminence of His returning into our every heart, that it shall not be a distant, far horizon to us, but it shall be near at hand, that already we shall live in that glory; already within our inmost being we shall dwell in the presence of that eternal morning. Our hearts hunger after righteousness, our souls hunger after Christ, and above all we desire that the church shall be ready in that day, and every life whom You would add to the body of believers shall be safely within the fold and ready on that day for that glorious coming. O the joy of that day when with unsullied garments of righteousness we stand before our beloved Christ, and we know our Saviour, and we know our Lord. O arise, church of Christ: awake and put on your beautiful garments, for lo, the light has risen upon you. When darkness covers the earth, His glory shall be seen in the church of Christ. O arise to the glory of that high calling, for Christ Himself is coming to meet you; Christ Himself is coming for His own. Be open in your being to the glory of that advent. Let the Son of God have the desire of His heart in your soul's free choosing of Him as the first beloved in your life. Oh, blessed be the name of the Lord. Father God Almighty, bring Your glory down to each of us, and let Your word prevail amongst us, for Jesus' precious name's sake.

Revive Thy Work

O LORD, revive Thy work in the midst of the years, In the midst of the years make it known; in wrath remember mercy (Hab 3:2).

I want to make it clear that I am not interested in conducting a merely academic exercise in studying the subject of revival. Rather I wish to examine it with a view to our experiencing it. Over recent months I have become

aware that there has been coming an intensifying presence of the Lord in our gatherings. I am aware of this in
my own spirit, but I also have regular reports from others,
and it is obvious that many are experiencing an unusual
sense of the presence of God. Frequently power comes
particularly strongly towards the end of our weekly Saturday night gatherings.[1] As we worship there is a sense of
divine power and divine presence. There has been
instantaneous healing. In such a moment there can come
that touch of God without any human ministry at all. It is
a visitation of God. Now I have been aware for a long time
that God is minded to bring revival to this land. I watch
carefully for the first signs of it. And remember, when
revival comes, there is a sense of divine presence, a recog-
nition of the presence of God, a feeling of God in the
atmosphere, a sensing of God and of the action of God
amongst men.

In these circumstances it seems to me wise to look at
revival in time past, to learn some of the principles and
the laws that govern it, so that in the hour of His visitation, we may have some knowledge of what to expect.
When we know what has happened in other times and
lands, we can be encouraged to prepare ourselves for the
falling of the great rain that will assuredly come upon our
own land, and that, I believe, before too long.

I opened the series with some thoughts on Charles G.
Finney in connection with revival, and I feel that I should
put a little addendum on to that before I move on to our
next study.

Finney's Calling and Gift

Finney taught that you can have revival when you want
to, that if you are prepared to fulfil the conditions govern-
ing revival, it will come as assuredly as will a harvest if a
farmer sows the seed in accordance with the laws of
nature.

Through the years between Finney's day and ours, many people have read and studied him, and have, in varying degrees, sought to promote revival: many a revival can trace its source to his teachings. But I suggest there was something that Finney overlooked, something that Wigglesworth in a later day overlooked, something that many people fail to understand: namely, the crucial role of individual gift and calling. Finney, for example, was called of God with a peculiar calling. To my mind he was a very apostle of revival. When he went into an area and powerful conviction fell, he seems not always to have been conscious of the component that he himself brought to the situation. He taught the principles of revival as he saw them, and revival surely followed. Others have attempted to do the same, and not always with quite the same degree of success. In Wigglesworth's case there is a similar situation. He exercised faith and taught the principles of faith as he understood them and he was amazingly used of God. He seems not always to have been aware of the part he himself played, or of the significance of the particular gifts God had given him. No mere artificial imitation can achieve the same results.

These truths came sharply to my mind many years ago. Once in London I had the privilege of hearing the late Principal George Jeffreys in a comparatively small meeting in Clapham. It was a normal Sunday morning communion service, not part of a campaign, and Mr Jeffreys was not in a prominent role until near the end of the service when communion was about to be taken. I have never forgotten the occasion. He stood there and spoke quietly of healing, quoting one or two scriptures. Suddenly the atmosphere became full of healing. One could feel healing, and indeed I remember thinking it would have been more difficult not to believe in it than it was to believe. This man was much used in that particular ministry. He had powerful gifts of healings — or to express it more accurately, God moved powerfully through him in healing.

I can imagine many aspiring young preachers being mightily impressed by Mr Jeffreys and anxious to emulate him. They could have addressed other companies as he had done on that occasion: 'The Lord is present to heal,' and been quite unable to bring the same atmosphere, or experience the same results. Mr Jeffreys had been endowed by God for his particular ministry, and without similar gift and calling their efforts could be quite unavailing.

I want to underline this by giving you some kind of indication of the man that Finney was and of his calling and of the effect of his presence and his preaching. It can be seen from two incidents.

A Factory Visit

The first is recorded by Finney without naming himself as the person concerned. He had gone into a factory to see the machinery:

> His mind was solemn, as he had been where there was a revival. The people who laboured there all knew him by sight, and knew who he was. A young lady who was at work saw him, and whispered some foolish remark to her companion, and laughed. The person stopped; her thread broke — and she was so much agitated that she could not join it. She looked out at the window to compose herself, and then tried again; again and again she strove to recover her self-command. At length she sat down, overcome by her feelings. [He] then approached and spoke with her; she soon manifested a deep sense of sin. The feeling spread through the establishment like fire, and in a few hours almost every person employed there was under conviction; so much so that the owner, though a worldly man, was astounded, and requested to have the works stopped and a prayer-meeting held; for he said it was a great deal more important to have these people converted than to have the works go on.[2]

An editor's footnote explains further:

[He said:] 'Stop the mill and let the people attend to religion'...the gates were closed, the factory stopped, and the meeting held forthwith. Finney's brother-in-law, who was superintendent of the factory, had invited the evangelist to the neighbourhood, and a crowded meeting had been held the previous night in the village school-house. Most of the young people from the factory had been present, and many had come under deep conviction. When, therefore, Finney visited the factory next morning they needed only a word to lead them to immediate decision for Christ.[3]

One man carried the anointing: powerful was the effect on the people.

Another Sodom

In the second example we read of a

remarkable instance of Divine leading in the choice of a subject and the management of a meeting which occurred in Finney's experience...In the outskirts of Antwerp, N.Y., where no religious services were usually held, he preached on the escape of Lot from Sodom. It so happened that the place was commonly called 'Sodom,' and the one pious man of the neighbourhood (who had invited Finney) was known as 'Lot.' Finney was entirely unaware of this, but the people, imagining him to have chosen the subject deliberately, in order to reproach them, were full of fury. In the end, however, there was an extraordinary breakdown, under the influence of the Spirit. Penitent sinners began to fall upon their knees in every direction, crying to God for mercy. 'If I had had a sword in each hand, I could not have cut them down so fast as they fell,' said Finney. The meeting continued all night, and in the morning (the building being required for school purposes) was adjourned to a private house, Finney renewing his labours in the afternoon. Years after, a minister who called upon him in order to give a donation of a hundred dollars to Oberlin College, proved to be one of the converts from that school-house meeting.[4]

Endued with power, given this glorious ministry, he found glorious results.

Warning on Introspection

There is one other footnote I want to put in about Finney, particularly for those of you who begin to read his lectures on revival. I have quoted a list of the sins of commission and omission which he recommended for our attention. Now I remember the effect on me when I first read that chapter, and I have known of its effect on others. He advises you to take a notebook and mark down where you are guilty, and you will find, as he himself indicates, that the act of remembering and writing down particular sins will bring others to mind. When you have gone through your list you should go through it again, and again. I tell you, if it wasn't so serious it could be quite funny. You start with maybe one or two pages of foolscap, and you rapidly require many more. If you do not believe me, try it. (As I speak I see one lady whom I'll not embarrass by naming: I don't know how many pages of foolscap she needed before she was finished. Indeed, I'm not sure that she ever was finished!)

Now the effect of this can be very salutary on people who are living carelessly, and who have very little thought of God. But on the other hand there are people who are naturally very introspective, who look in and begin to try to sort the sins of a lifetime, and find themselves coming into terrible bondage. For that reason I have been careful through the years in lending Finney's *Revival Lectures* and in recommending how people should handle it. I want to make this very clear to you. It is not you, nor your neighbour, nor a preacher, evangelist or writer who is ultimately responsible for bringing a consciousness of your sin to your heart. We read of the Holy Spirit, that He *will convict the world in respect of sin, and of righteousness, and of judgement...he shall take of mine, and shall declare it unto you* (Jn 16:8, 14). And I can assure you that if you are honest with God, you can trust the Holy Spirit to begin to reveal to you things that are blocking your getting through to God, barriers that must be broken down, sins under the surface that must come to the light and be put away. The Holy Spirit brings such to your remembrance. You come to a place where you don't go on digging, and you don't search any more. You become totally open to the revelation of the Holy Spirit, and in no legalistic way do you seek forgiveness, or strive for it by any works; but under His anointing, under His revelation, you meet the terms that God is laying down for your individual life. You do what you are told. It may lead ultimately to deep dying, but it may not initially. And God sets you free; many a deep-dyed sinner has been set free in a few moments of time by the blessed application of the blood of the Lord Jesus. I want to leave you with balanced teaching so that you do not act carelessly but rather look to see what may be coming between you and God. Neither should you become over-introspective, trying by the work of your own hand, as it were, to make amends with God. *The blood of Jesus his Son cleanseth from all sin* (1 Jn 1:7).

Notes

1 Our Saturday night meetings are attended by people from many parts of Scotland.
2 Charles G. Finney, *Revival Lectures*, pp. 10–11.
3 Ibid., pp. 11–12, note.
4 Ibid., p. 130, note.

3 | THE METHODIST REVIVAL

We come now across the Atlantic to our own land. Slightly earlier than the movement with Finney in America, there came the glorious revival associated with the Wesleys and Whitefield and the early Methodists. I want to give you a little background and a little understanding of a spiritual principle before we look at detail.

The Darkest Hour Before the Dawn

There is part of a verse in Isaiah that is sometimes rendered, *when the adversary shall come in like a flood, the spirit of the LORD shall lift up a standard against him* (Is 59:19, RV margin). May I say that frequently the darkest hour comes before the dawn. Think for a moment of the darkness of Calvary, the darkness around that cross, the spiritual darkness across the face of the land. Do you realize that this was within a matter of hours of the resurrection of the Lord Jesus and the breaking of one of the brightest days on earth? The darkest hour came before the dawning. And you will find frequently in your own experience that the dark hours come most intensely before the coming of light. Be encouraged: it is almost a law of life.

There came an hour in Britain that was one of the darkest in the history of the nation. I remember in school days we had a textbook which described eighteenth century England (and here I mean England, not Britain) just

41

prior to the Wesleyan revival. The book had a series of headings, each using the word 'nadir' (which means lowest point, or dark night) to portray the age. One referred to the nadir of religion — an age when many ministers were unconverted. It was a polished age, with a very marked attitude against 'enthusiasm', as they called much that we would regard as proper and normal in our religion. There was a great deadness and darkness in spiritual life. It was indeed the nadir of religion.

It was the nadir of national life: an age of corruption. Parliament was corrupt and institutions were corrupt. It was the nadir of social life: an age of drunkenness, violence, smuggling and dishonesty. About 160 offences were punishable by death. An age of debauchery and cruel, grinding poverty, it was indeed a dark, dark night in England. It was the nadir of the arts. Indeed it was an age of nadirs. I was myself a history student and teacher, and like many of you, probably, had a normal schoolboy's introduction to history, which consisted largely in the learning of facts culled from scholars whose original work or sources we never saw. It was a kind of second-hand experience, and had little to do with 'real' history or original documents. But I remember finding my own way around a library and beginning to read more authentic history, where I got much nearer the actual events of Wesley's day. In one particularly graphic presentation of the period, the writer included contemporary placards. These depicted an age when drunkenness was extremely rife. Outside the pubs they used to have notices like the following printed: 'Drunk for a penny; dead drunk, twopence; straw supplied.' That wasn't an attempt at humour; that was just life as it was. Such a placard gave me a real insight into that age, an age of debauchery.

A Standard Raised

Now God was minded to lift up a standard against over-flowing wickedness. And He put His hand on a small group of men. They had a mind to know God and to serve God, but at first they didn't know salvation. They began to live very strictly, trying to follow God's laws to the best of their ability. In due time they all found salvation. Prominent in this group were John and Charles Wesley and George Whitefield. They knew the real joy of passing from death into life. God began to move through them, and the country was turned upside down. An age of formal religion and lax preaching was rocked to its foundations. They started their work intending to remain within the Church, but they found what many another has found, that new wine bursts old bottles, and old institutions cannot always contain the new life that comes welling up in revival times. They were almost forced to preach in the open air. Indoors pulpits were shut to them, but there were open pulpits in the fields, and the people gathered by thousands and tens of thousands, up to perhaps thirty thousand at a time. The power of the mighty God came down upon these men. Their voices were like the sound of trumpets, and the anointing of the living God was upon them. Men and women came in vast numbers and were born of God. Mighty power flowed and many went down prostrate during the preaching, crying to God for salvation.

There in Bristol the tears of the miners flowed, making rivulets in their blackened faces as they joyfully heard the word of God and turned in vast numbers to God. These early Methodists were hated, they were opposed, they were persecuted, they were shamefully treated; but they had faces like the faces of lions, they had courage that was almost incredible. John Wesley lived to the age of eighty-seven. As an old man of eighty-four he preached four sermons a day and travelled by horseback eighty miles a day; sometimes he walked thirty miles a day. He lived in great frugality all the days of his life; he died with hardly a penny left. He gave and gave and gave. Unhappy in his marriage, he had a wife who is said to have pulled him across the floor by the hairs of his venerable head...and some have said he was maybe glad to get out to preach! (Maybe if some wives in the twentieth century treated their husbands similarly it would waken them up and get them out too!) However that may be, Wesley and his ilk were powerful men of God.

Opposition of Hell

I want to bring to you one episode. You will appreciate that when Wesley, for example, went into a community and began to preach, he emptied the public houses, he emptied the dens of vice, he took away the trade of those who were dealing in vice. It is as though he came into Glasgow and all the drug addiction was broken, and all the drug addicts came to Christ. There would be great resistance from those with a vested interest in the sale of drugs. In Wesley's day word passed from town to town about his coming, and his enemies were often waiting for him with sticks and stones. Sometimes they actually tried to kill him. The following extracts are taken from John Pollock's vivid account of Wesley's adventures in Staffordshire in 1743.[1]

...Egginton [vicar of Wednesbury] and his curate at Darlaston, and the vicar of Walsall, were determined to destroy the society. They spread word among roughs and bruisers in their parishes that cock-fighting, bull-baiting and prize fights were in danger; the local magistrates were persuaded to turn a blind eye.

In May Charles came...and was knocked about by a violent crowd. That summer, Methodists had windows broken and houses, shops and workshops shamelessly looted; they were beaten and splattered with mud. 'Some,' [said Wesley] 'even pregnant women, were treated in a manner that cannot be mentioned' (*John Wesley*, p. 169).

A few months later Wesley himself arrived. He did not run away from it. We read that he faced a larger congregation than anticipated, and preached on *Jesus Christ, the same yesterday, and today, and forever*. He said, 'I believe everyone present felt the power of God: and no creature offered to molest us, either going or coming; but the Lord fought for us, and we held our peace' (p. 170).

But during the afternoon as he was writing,

> A number of Methodists were in the house...Suddenly they heard the horn which summoned the roughs. Soon an agitated Methodist cried out that a mob surrounded the house. Wesley calmly announced that they would pray. They knelt round him as he and then others prayed extempore. The howls and threats outside died down until within half an hour, when someone looked out of the door, 'not a man was left'.
>
> Wesley suggested he had better leave as the mob was after him rather than them, but they begged him to stay. He foresaw the result.
>
> About five the mob was back in greater force — it came from Darlaston, where the mines were...Wesley could hear the cry, 'Bring out the minister! We'll have the minister!' He told a frightened Methodist to go to the front door and bring in the ringleader, 'by the hand' (p. 170).

This was done, a few sentences were interchanged, and the lion became like a lamb.

> Wesley told him to fetch one or two more and he brought a man and a woman, both in a rage; 'but in two minutes they were as calm as he'.
>
> Wesley then went to the door, stood on a chair, and the crowd quietened.... He spoke a few words about the love of God, and the mob cheered. The woman ringleader cried out, 'the gentleman is an honest gentleman, and we will spill our blood in his defence!' (pp. 170–1).

Then he was taken to the magistrate, who was in bed and not to be roused, and it seemed that things were going to be fine. But at that point a mob from a neighbouring town who were natural enemies of these folks came:

...a great mob roared up out of Walsall. Wesley found himself caught in the midst of gang warfare between traditional enemies. 'The Darlaston mob made what defence they could; but they were weary, as well as out-numbered: so that in a short time, many being knocked down, the rest ran away, and left me in their hands.' The Darlaston collier woman who had sworn to defend him charged the Walsall mob 'and knocked down three or four men, one after another. But many assaulting her at once, she was soon overpowered, and had probably been killed in a few minutes (three men keeping her down and beating her with all their might), had not a man called to one of them, "Hold, Tom, hold!" '

.   .   .   .

The screaming mob pulled Wesley [and others]...towards Walsall, down the steep and wet cobbled street: one slip and he would have gone down and they would have pummelled him to death; but he kept his feet, with his heart at peace. Several blows with bludgeons were deflected, he knew not how, except that his small size made him a difficult target in a mêlée. And one man who 'came rushing through the press, and raising his arm to strike, on a sudden let it drop, and only stroked my head, saying, "What soft hair he has!" '

.   .   .   .   .   .

Wesley shouted, 'Will you hear me?'

'No, no! Knock his brains out! Kill him!'

'What evil have I done? Which of you have I wronged?' He began to speak of the love of God and they listened. He spoke for a quarter of an hour, when his voice failed.

The mob, led by Honest Munchin the prize fighter, roared again, 'Bring him away! Strip him!'

'You needn't do that: I will give you my clothes.'

'Crucify him!' — Wesley was sure he heard the words.

His voice then recovered and he began to pray aloud as if oblivious of anyone but Christ. Suddenly the prize-fighter turned to him: 'Sir, I will spend my life for you: follow me, and not one soul here shall touch a hair of your head.' Two or three others said likewise...

...but before they could cross the footbridge at the mill dam the mob began to bay for his blood again. 'Throw him in,' cried some. The threat did not bother Wesley: he could swim. [But a Methodist woman was thrown in.]

A man hit him on the mouth and nose. The blood gushed but Wesley felt no pain and all at once realized why the martyrs had died so calmly in the flames.

.   .   .   .

Next day...Wesley rode out towards Nottingham, bruised but happy...'He *looked* like a soldier of Christ' [wrote his brother Charles]. 'His clothes were torn to tatters' (pp. 171-3).

Charles later asked the riot leader, who became one of the Methodists and a leader in the area, what he thought of John Wesley.

' "Think of him!" said he: "that he is a man of God. And God was on his side, when so many of us could not kill one man." ' 'Munchin' Clifton became a pillar of the Methodists of Wednesbury and Walsall...until his death, aged eighty-five, forty-six years later (p. 173).

No French Revolution in Britain

The power of God was with the men of His choosing. He turned the country upside down. It is considered by many historians that the result of the work of the Wesleys and Whitefield and the early Methodists was such that it prevented a revolution in Britain similar to the French Revolution, which was one fearful bloodbath. It is reckoned that the country was saved from that as a result of the work of these men: in other words, by the coming of revival.

Almost all the forward progress of the church of Christ can be related to revival or the effects of revival. Many in our own company have been affected by a stream flowing out from the 1904 revival in Wales and coming to these

parts through the late George Jeffreys. It affected some
lives very deeply in 1929, and consequently the lives of
the next generation.

A Recurring Pattern

I want to show you a pattern which repeats through the
course of history. There is the grip of deep evil, the lifting
up of the standard of God, the downcoming of the power
of the Spirit, the new wine bursting the old bottles, a
movement such as the Methodist movement hoping to
remain within the national church, unable to do so, thrust
out, and a new movement of God born. Watch the progress: after revival and the spontaneous moving of God,
there comes a cooling-down process, followed by crystall-
ization, consolidation, and then a comparative death.

   In a later age, God wanted to move out in power again
amongst the needy, and he put his hand on William
Booth. Booth was a Methodist and intended to remain so,
but he found that the new wine burst the old bottle. There
in Nottingham he gathered a number of outcasts, desperately needy people, clad in garments that smelled fear-
fully. He took them into the Methodist church. And
people were not happy to sit beside them — any happier
than we might have been, let us be fair. Booth knew when
the day came that he had to go outside the church, and the
Salvation Army was born. And make no mistake about it:
that movement in its early days was a movement of power
and glory, wonderfully used of God, bringing thousands
of souls to Christ. But, you know, after the initial stages of
burning revival, there comes the cooling down, the
institutionalizing, the consolidation, the comparative
death. Again and again within the Salvation Army God
has raised people, in our own day, baptized people in the
Holy Spirit — and not all of them have found it easy, I
think, to remain within the Salvation Army. This is the
process: a recurring pattern.

And we are part of that pattern, because there dawned a day when there came a Pentecostal outburst, with glory flowing in many directions. Watch the cooling down, the crystallizing, and the dying. I remember the leader of one Pentecostal church telling me, 'There is a danger that comes in the third generation. The first generation know the mighty actions of God. The second generation have a memory of them. And the third generation have forgotten or never known.' And it is so true. Then God has to burst out again.

The Power of the Class Meeting

I want to touch on other two issues. One of the ways in which the Methodist revival carried on in considerable power was not merely the great mass meetings that were held, nor the regular meetings of the societies that were formed, but also the class meetings, which involved the dividing of the company into smaller groups, maybe of a dozen, or sometimes rather more. They met and had deep Christian fellowship. They opened up their lives to each other, they shared their experiences, and they confessed their sins one to another. There was a great openness and a great sincerity, and a going on deeply with God. And I am interested to see that in our own day increasingly, in some circles including our own, while there are still mass gatherings, there is also a dividing into smaller companies for more intimate fellowship and teaching.

Confession of Sin

Now here I want to put in a little word of caution. Confession of sin is enjoined by the Bible: *Is any among you sick? let him call for the elders of the church...and if he have committed sins, it shall be forgiven him. Confess therefore your sins one to another, and pray one for another* (Jas 5:14–16). I have found through the years that there are times when people coming for counsel have to confess their sins. I often say, 'So far as I am concerned, if you get clear with God I am not particularly anxious to hear of your sins.' But in many cases they do not feel they can really be free from their troubles until they speak about them, and that is in order. In revival meetings again and again the power of God has so come on people that they have been forced to confess publicly.

But, you know, the devil can get in as well, and you can have public confession of sin which is harmful and ought not to be public. Sexual deviation is a particular danger area. I want again to strike a balanced note. If you have sinned and you go before God, He is faithful and just to forgive you your sin. If you find that you are not getting through and you need help, go to someone whom you totally trust to retain a confidence, and receive the necessary help. But do not postpone having sin dealt with till revival comes, lest the sin come pouring out publicly in a flood. You will not be able to stand the pollution of it in the hour of God's power. There is a place for private confession, to God alone or to man. There is a place for public confession, particularly if the sin has been of a public nature. Sometimes without this an individual is never fully forgiven by a company. On the other hand, unwise confession, for example, of deep uncleanness, in a mixed company may be positively harmful and should not be allowed. There is also a danger of focusing too much attention on weaknesses and problems. All should be done, and only be done, under the leading of the Holy Spirit.

Enduring Principles of Revival

Finally, as we study revival you will find that there are certain underlying principles, certain things that are common to all revivals. You might hear people using careless language: 'Oh, this is a revival of joy,' 'This is a revival of praise,' 'This is a revival of love.' Now you will get joy, and you will get praise, and you will get love accompanying revival after the breakthrough has come. But revival basically deals with sin. The coming of the power of God into the life of an individual, or of a company, brings conviction. The first thing that normally accompanies God-consciousness is a consciousness of sin. It is sin that causes the barrier between man and God. And you will not have the full flood of the life of God while sin is under the carpet. Sin causes the trouble, and indeed it is sometimes sin that prevents you becoming physically whole, never mind spiritually whole. You will never be fully happy with covered sin. When God comes to us, sin is stirred up and dealt with. That is my call to you now. Whether you picture yourself back in a Finney-type revival, or in a Methodist-type revival, or in any other type of revival, there is no real revival that will let you off with sin. There is no hiding-place, there is no covering-place, there is no place of escape. As the Holy One draws near, you become conscious of unforgiven sin, you repent and seek forgiveness. Then the gracious Spirit applies the blood of Jesus, and the blood of Jesus cleanses from all sin. Let the power of the blood touch you, cleanse you. I am not asking you to go and make an endless search. The Holy Spirit Himself reveals what is needed.

And if on an earlier occasion God has forgiven your sin, don't go and dig it up again. I sometimes illustrate this from the behaviour of a typical dog. He gets a bone, and he deals faithfully with the bone, but he can't consume it altogether. Ultimately he buries what is left of it in the garden for a rainy day. Normally he forgets where he has buried it, but occasionally, maybe a month later, he either remembers or accidentally comes on it and digs it up. By that time the bone is something else. And Fido acts strangely. It is not enough for him to sniff it and pass by: he digs it up, and then he rolls on it. I don't know what the purpose of the rolling is, but dogs do it through their generations: they roll on it, and they roll on it, and maybe they think that you want to share the benefit of the bone. In they come, and the whole house smells with the smell of the stinking bone. You know, I meet Christians whose sins have been buried in the sea of God's forgetfulness, but again they have remembered them, and they dig them up and they roll on them, and they roll on them. Please don't do it. Let's deal only with the sins that the Holy Spirit is bringing to your consciousness, and you'll find that *He is faithful and righteous to forgive us our sins, and to cleanse us from all unrighteousness* (1 Jn 1:9). It may be that into your memory, into your consciousness has come the conviction of unforgiven sin, a sense that all is not well between you and God, and you want it taken out of the way. Take time to let the word sink in. Revival means cleansing from sin. Come and, like Naaman of old, wash and be clean. If your heart has been touched, and you have become conscious of sin-stains by the way, let the blood touch you. Come to faith. God is not mocked, but neither does He torment His people. If He convicts of sin, it is with the purpose of having it put away, not that you go on carrying it. Be rid of it, be done with it. Let the blood cleanse.

> EXHORTATION [MB]: *Christ is looking for a Bride, the church of Christ, who shall be wholly His in the day of His coming. Surely the choice you make now in the morning time of your life, when the choices still lie before you for the ultimate direction that life shall take — surely now is a crucial time. Christ would reveal Himself to you as the supreme desire of your heart, as the supreme home of your soul, as the supreme love which will govern your way. He has been knocking, knocking, knocking upon your heart for a fuller and a deeper entrance, that you might make Him your choice. Remember Rebekah: she faced a desert crossing, and the leaving of her home and kindred, to marry one she had not seen, called Isaac, and she was asked, 'Wilt thou go with this man?' — the*

*man who was sent to bring her to the bridegroom. So
the voice of the Holy Spirit entreats you... 'Wilt thou
go? Wilt thou obey the call?' No other thing on that
horizon, no other attraction but the single voice of
Christ, calling you from your own kith and kin and
kindred, from the ways that you have known, across a
desert, maybe, into the arms of Christ, His certainty
before your soul. 'O child of Mine, wilt thou go with
this man?'*

Note

[1] John Pollock, *John Wesley* (Lion Publishing, 1992).

4 | MATTERS RELATED TO REVIVAL

PRELIMINARY REMARKS: *A sense of the weight of the Holy Spirit is with us — and people don't always quite understand how to react. Some might feel we should burst out in an exuberant way, but there is a restraining power with us, the power of God. As we gathered tonight there was a silence which I greatly welcomed. Not a voice was heard. As we came into worship there was a deepening of that brooding sense.*

It took me back to the breath of revival that I knew at a school camp away back, almost forty years ago. God had broken out in power overnight, and hundreds of pupils were gathered in the assembly hall in the morning. There was a silence, and a brooding — and a headmaster who knew nothing of these things. I remember his saying something of this sort: 'I'm not impressed with the sombre look that is on your faces!' A mass of souls were facing God, and there was no levity, there was no nonsense, no pranks, no practical joking. The sense of God.

It also took me back to many a day on the island of Lewis. When the people gathered for house meetings in the aftermath of revival you went in, and nobody spoke; you sat down, and nobody spoke. You became aware of God, the vast deeps of God. When revival comes, people become God-conscious, not man-conscious. He breaks the hearts of men and He remakes us according to His own fashion. I feel the glory of the draw of revival on my soul now. Blessed be His name.

The opposition of hell has come on this series of studies. Satan has been attacking in various ways. But something rather remarkable has happened since we began. I have just had evidence of revival breaking out in Minnesota this year with Ian Andrews. I will not go into detail about this at the moment, but I am convinced that by the end of this series you will not only believe that God moved in revival in time past, but you will believe that God can move in revival now; and I can assure you that in some places He is actually doing it now. I trust that most of you will believe that it will happen in our own land. God is beginning to stir the embers even now.

One thing I learned deeply at that school camp so long ago: the Holy Spirit does more in a few minutes of time than we could do in many lifetimes, more in fact than we can ever do. Young people and adults are broken by the power of the Holy Spirit and remade in great power and glory. Prepare your hearts for the coming of God. Did you want to come to a 'happy, clappy' meeting? Ultimately a revival meeting is the happiest kind of meeting you will probably ever know on earth. But it will not be happy with surface froth.

Revival will touch your deepest chords and change you for time and eternity.

*Blessed be His name. His presence is more
manifest now, I believe, than it has been
for many days.*

PRAYER: *Lord, no matter how often Thou
hast been present and anointed preaching,
we can never take this for granted or come
in any measure in our own strength. We
pray that there shall come deep
illumination from the throne of glory, a
deep understanding of the ways of God
with man, a deep revelation of the heart of
man and the heart of Christ. Be with us, O
God, in power, we ask. In His name and for
His sake, Amen.*

Age-abiding and Transient Aspects of Revival

I want to remind you again that this series of addresses on
revival is not intended to become a merely academic
exercise nor, in publishing, merely to add to academic
theses. As we look into the past, I want us to learn some of
the deep lessons of revival that are applicable to our own
day. You will find that there are principles which are age-
abiding: they never change. But there are various aspects
of revival that are peculiar to particular times and places,
and are not always repeated.

There is a danger in our trying to produce revival in the
twentieth century by taking models from earlier ages, not
realizing that while certain principles are unchanging,
there are variations peculiar to time and place, not univer-
sally applicable and not necessarily appropriate now.
These things are age-abiding: the need for repentance, the
fact of conviction of sin, a knowledge of coming judgment, an awareness of the reality of hell, followed by the
wonderful revelation of the power of Christ to save.

Repentance, Judgment, Hell

As soon as a revival passes, men begin to nibble at the edges of the severe doctrines. Regarding repentance — well, it's natural (they say) for man to sin, to step aside. Surely 'to err is human', and we must be tolerant of people's wrongdoing. Softer words are used for sin, and there is a blurring of the edges of basic truth. Gradually the very word *repentance* falls out of use. Do you know that prior to Billy Graham's coming to Britain in the middle of this century the word 'repentance' in gospel preaching had almost been forgotten? 'Opportunity for decision' was on every hand. A cheap believism was widely proclaimed. Suddenly there came a man under the anointing of God who told men and women clearly that they were sinners in need of salvation. They became aware that they were in danger of hell. I noticed in these early days in Kelvin Hall in Glasgow that on the nights on which Billy preached about the broken law, the broken commandments, and brought sin sharply to the consciousness of the multitude, they responded in great numbers. This was no cheap believism; this was encounter with the living God, and sin was uncovered and forgiven.

Now as revival fades,[1] the doctrine of sin tends to slip under the carpet. And judgment: well, who has a right to judge? As for God — He's a God of love, and we can't believe that such a God would judge and send people to an endless torment. My friend, why do you think of God sending anybody to torment? Don't you think that men go there in spite of God and all that God has done for them on Calvary?

I remember the late Duncan Campbell telling me that as he had preached these fundamental doctrines in the country parts of Lewis, and revival had shaken many parts of the island, the time came for him to preach in Stornoway. Now Stornoway was perhaps a hundred years more backward than the country parts. You say, what do you mean — are you not making a mistake there? Oh, no, I know that the world would have viewed the island of Lewis as perhaps a hundred years behind the Mainland, and Stornoway in a middle position, less so. But I don't view it that way. The country parts were a hundred years nearer God than was the Mainland, and Stornoway was partly contaminated by the Mainland — let me put it bluntly — more modern, more up-to-date, more sophisticated. Duncan Campbell thought, 'I can't preach exactly the same in Stornoway as I have been doing in the country parts.' When Duncan Campbell preached on hell, I gather that nobody who heard it was ever likely to forget it. As one old Highland woman, a Bible believer, said: 'The hell of the Bible, it is terrible. But oh, the hell of Duncan Campbell!' She had heard hell preached by Duncan Campbell under the anointing of the Holy Spirit, and it had gripped her, and she knew the reality of it as she had never known it before.

He thought, 'I can't go into Stornoway and preach as I preach in the country parts.' And God said in effect: 'The message is the same message.' He preached it, and God moved in Stornoway. And I know he tried to preach it in parts of the south, and in England particularly he was resisted to his face by certain leading evangelicals. You will know of the heresy that has come in ever more strongly now amongst some of our brethren, with their ultimate reconciliation views and a scenario which does not include hell. A departure from some of the deep fundamentals of the faith was showing long back. The doctrine of hell was hated. Luke 16 with its teaching had become inconvenient in today's world. Let me point out and underline one thing for you: they had revival in Lewis, and they did not have it in the modernistic parts of the evangelical world, nor, I believe, will they ever have it, without receiving the fundamental, unchanging, age-enduring truths of conviction, repentance, and eternal judgment. The Holy Spirit convicts of sin, righteousness and judgment to come, He leads into *all* truth: He makes a thorough job of cleansing the church.

Now these things are abiding and enduring. But there are outward sides of revival, more peripheral aspects that are related to the age and generation and the people concerned, which are not in vogue in every revival. I want you to see that division and that difference right from the beginning, as we learn lessons from the past.

Can the Tide of Wickedness be Turned?

I have spoken of Wesley and the Methodist revival. I want to continue with that for a little before moving on. There is one interesting point that has caught my attention. You know how you can be terribly distressed when you look out at the sin that is abounding all around. I have said before, and am prepared to repeat, that there is a difference between what you believe at a mind level and what you believe in your spirit. I remember having a terrible consciousness of the depth of iniquity that is sweeping the country and is indeed often in the church itself. The idea that God will pour out revival and change all of that, change these thugs, these murderers, these rapists, can seem so improbable. You can hardly touch your daily paper without being aware of the flood of vileness and filth that is sweeping the land. Fairly recently I faced the question, 'Do you really believe that God is going to change this?' And you know, in my spirit I didn't. Oh, I would have said, 'Yes, I believe God can do anything.' But this was at a mind level. Away deep down in my spirit I did not *really* believe it.

And you know, God in His mercy caused me to consider one moment of the power of God. I have seen that sweeping, glorious power before which men go down like corn before the reaper. Who shall abide His coming? Who shall stand in the day of the Lord, in the day of the power of the Lord? His coming is in glory, and He is a refiner of silver. Mountains flow down at His presence.

I realized I had been looking in the wrong direction. When you look at sin you become depressed and your faith can fail. But in that one moment of revelation I suddenly knew, 'Lord, all that is needed is the release of the power of the living God.' *For, behold, the day cometh, it burneth as a furnace; and all the proud, and all that work wickedness, shall be stubble: and the day that cometh shall burn them up* (Mal 4:1). And in my heart and in my spirit I believed God, and I believe God now. I believe He will turn, turn and overturn (Eze 21:27), and the glory and the power of God will flow again in this land: glory be to His holy name! Where wickedness comes in like a flood, the Spirit of the Lord lifts up a standard against him, O blessed be His name!

In this context a friend raised an interesting point. She had noticed that the wickedness of Britain in the eighteenth century, as I had described it in relation to the Methodist revival, was intense. It may actually have been worse than present wickedness, great as this is — although you might find that difficult to believe. The wickedness in Britain in those days was horrendous. This actually encouraged my friend. I think she suddenly saw that if God did what He did in the Britain of that day, it could happen again. Instead of being depressed by the present state, she was encouraged by God's earlier action in the face of hell. If God moved into the pit of iniquity in Wesley's day, He can move into the pit of iniquity in Britain in the twentieth century. I want you to find faith strengthening as we ponder revival and related themes.

John Wesley's Exertions

As I have already indicated, Wesley laboured for half a century, dying in his late eighties. He would read and study as he rode on horseback, and at the end of his journey, fresh as a daisy, he would preach — on average, fifteen sermons a week. He covered a quarter of a million miles, up and down and across the land — England, Scotland, Wales, Ireland — and in America too. He believed in working as hard as he could, saving as much as he could, and giving away all that he could. He lived a life that would put me to shame, an incredible life. Cruelly disappointed in one lady whom he had hoped to marry, and thereafter exceedingly unhappy in his marriage to another, he went on with God in power. I touched on some of the violence he encountered, and this shocked some of you. Read the full story, for I only showed you the tip of the iceberg. He was assaulted again and again, escaping with his life when his enemies wanted to kill him.

Calvinism and Arminianism

There are three things I want to speak of before I move on from Wesley and revival in that day — because I want you to go beyond the bare facts of history, to ponder principles related to the movement, and some of the difficulties encountered. There came for Wesley a real problem with the Moravians at a fairly early stage when they would have quenched some of the fire in his meetings and produced an undue quietism. He resisted that successfully, while retaining a real love for the Moravians, who had been instrumental in bringing him to Christ. But later there came intense trouble which split the developing movement over an issue which has caused division through the ages: the problem of reconciling the doctrine of election with that of human effort. In philosophy a similar problem arises: the reconciliation of determinism with free will.

Whitefield was possibly one of the greatest preachers who ever preached in Britain, a very lovable and saintly man, and he was a Calvinist, strongly emphasizing election. Wesley too was a mighty preacher and one of the greatest organizers as well as one of the saintliest of men, and he was an opponent of any tendency to hyper-Calvinism. His insistence upon human freedom to respond to God caused some to think him an Arminian. (He was a born controversialist and perhaps sometimes unduly suspicious — though the latter could also be said of Whitefield on occasion.) Now I am not going to take an endless time going into the doctrines of predestination, election, free grace, Calvinism, Arminianism: you can ponder these topics at your own leisure.[2] But I will make a few observations. First let me put my cards on the table. I believe that in the dealings of God with the soul, the first movement comes from God, but that it is our privilege and responsibility to respond. This may require divine enabling, but there is a part we have to play. I do not believe we can make God do anything. I do not believe that we have the means of grace under our own hand or under our own control. But having said that, I am a total opponent of hyper-Calvinism.

An Extreme Example

An occasion on the island of Lewis is imprinted on my mind. God had been with me as I went from house to house, and the Bible was speaking remarkably appositely about one condition after another in the lives of individuals. I was due to visit a lady who was suffering from some physical ailment. But my Bible spoke of nothing but salvation. You know how you can say, 'Oh, I wonder — I wonder — ' and yet you feel deeply that God is speaking to you about something your mind doesn't understand. I went and was obedient to the word of God, and spoke about salvation. And sure enough, I discovered that she came from an exceedingly hyper-Calvinistic background. There she was lying in bed, hoping that some day it would happen to her, that some day she would be converted.

'Oh, some day it will maybe happen to me!'

The power of God was with me, the clarity of the doctrine of salvation was there, and I presented the invitation of Christ that is for every sinner born. At the end, when it was so clear, so very clear, she still failed to grasp it. You know, when the Holy Spirit is there you can make the way of salvation clear; if He is not there your fingers are all thumbs and things are confused. But when Christ is there it is so clear. And it was very clear. Yet at the end of it, she said, 'Oh, it would be wonderful if it would happen to me.'

'But, my friend,' I said, 'it's here now, God is here now, He wants to take you now! Behold, now is the acceptable time, now is the day of salvation, now!'

'Oh, yes, it would be wonderful.'

And I left that poor soul with the words on her lips, 'It would be wonderful if some time it would happen to me too.' I could not shake her out of her hyper-Calvinism.

God's Part and Man's

Now Wesley feared that the line Whitefield was taking on election was leading to an extreme position, and he in turn strongly presented human responsibility rather than emphasizing election. In examining his statements, I judge him to have been moderate, and his teaching on election wholly acceptable. But you know how extreme positions can be taken. Not only are there hyper-Calvinists today, but there are what might be described as hyper-Arminians too.

You may sometimes read a book, or listen to some preachers, and almost feel that God has been left out.

'My friend, you can be born again tonight. You can find the Lord Jesus — just you raise your hand and fit your name into this part of John 3:16 and you can be saved tonight — whenever you like.'

My friend, you can't. You can't. Unless the Holy Spirit is moving, there is no salvation. Being born again is being born by the power of the Spirit. But having said all that, let me say this: God is far more interested in saving your soul than you are in being saved. You are starting from a background where God has given an invitation and God loves you. But still you don't do it yourself. You may only move in response to God: God has got to be in it. God has got to be there.

Now see the dangers of both sides. If you say to people, 'You can't be saved until God saves you,' they may say, 'Well, there is no point in me doing anything; I'll sit here and wait for something to happen. I'm going to be saved or lost anyway.' And on the other side there is the danger, 'I'll live as I like, and when I like I'll turn to God and I'll give my life to Christ,' as though it was in your hand to do this. Can you see the heresies and the dangers of both positions?

Finney's Position

I stand with Finney. I stand with Finney on many things. Finney was a great soul-winner, and a great reader of the hearts of men: a man of tremendous perception and wisdom. He would go into an area in America where they were Arminian in doctrine, where salvation was related to what *they* did. They depended largely on their works and had little conception of divine action or the need for divine initiative. Finney must have appeared to them as a dyed-in-the-wool Calvinist as he thundered: 'You are going to hell, unless you have a real meeting with the living God. Unless there is an action and a movement of the Holy Spirit, you are a lost soul.' He kicked the props from under them, he removed the coverings from over their heads, which were barriers to their souls' salvation.

They came under fearful conviction, and came to God in masses.

Then he would go into a Calvinistic area where the tune was different. 'If I belong to the elect, I'll be all right for ever. I will then be amongst the chosen. I never need to be urgent in spreading the gospel: it is all in God's hand; God will do as He wills. Those who are to be saved will be saved — those who are ordained to hell will go there. There is nothing I can do.'

So Finney took another line: he emphasized human responsibility. 'God has spoken. God has made provision. Now it is up to you! What have you done with the message that God has given you? How have you responded?' He emphasized the side of human responsibility — and people were left almost thinking it was all in their hands, and they got up from their lazy beds, and they got on with obeying God, and revival poured across their borders. You might almost have said he was an Arminian in one place and a Calvinist in the other. He was neither the one nor the other; he was a servant of the living God, and he expressed truth as I believe it to be in Jesus Christ. There is a place for divine action; there is also a place for human response.

Love in Spite of Doctrinal Differences

The controversy on the subject between Wesley and Whitefield split their movement. I want to say one thing about this. You will appreciate that I am now in a preaching rather than a teaching situation, which means that I may not go into fine detail night after night for weeks. I can only touch high points, and I want to emphasize one thing. While the issue caused a great deal of hurt and pain between these two men, they were both servants of the living God, they loved Christ, and they loved each other, and in spite of their doctrinal differences maintained, though maybe with brief intervals of difficulty, a very Christlike attitude to each other.[3]

Again if I may refer to Finney, he points out that in a revival it is not necessary to get all the churches in an area to be welded together. You will have trouble if you try to weld churches together. When he went into an area, he would not insist that the Baptists and the Presbyterians should change their fundamental doctrinal positions and become one people. What he did emphasize as essential was that they should maintain a spirit of love towards each other in spite of their differences. You will find, if we go forward into revival in Scotland, that God loves all His people — the Brethren, the Salvation Army, the Baptists, the Church of Scotland...He loves far more deeply than perhaps you imagine — and He loves even us! He wants to draw all men: *I, if I be lifted up from the earth, will draw all men unto myself* (Jn 12:32).

When revival burns like fire, so many people will come from all over the place that they will never all get in here, that's for sure! I don't know where we will meet, but they will never get in here when revival comes! It is less easy than it used to be to get a seat in the main part of the building now if you come late, and you will certainly not get in at all by arriving at the normal time when revival comes! People will gather from all over. And they will not be unduly interested in your tag, whether you're Pentecostal or otherwise. They will want God. People want God, people need God. Revival has a magnetic attraction. When people know that the living God is there, wild horses won't keep them away. And that doesn't mean that because love flows you swallow the errors of Rome, or that you swallow the errors of Canterbury, or the errors of some of our leading evangelicals who may be men much used in time past; nor do I assume that we have no errors of our own, which others may be unable to accept. But let love flow. Love all men and hope to be loved. Love your Roman Catholic friends. Let me say again: this does not mean that we should adopt any one of their heresies, any more than they should adopt any heresies that we may be holding. But love does cover.

Ah, you can feel Him. I know by your stillness you feel Him here (and I trust readers will feel Him too). The Holy One is in the midst of us, and He will read your hearts...the Holy One of Israel.

Understanding the Martyrs

Other two interesting footnotes about Wesley. Our reading included an incident where he had suffered violence, and he suddenly exclaimed that now he could understand the martyrs, for he felt no pain. That used to be a great mystery to me, how the martyrs went through their sufferings with the fortitude that they showed, the inflexible nature of their resolve in agonizing situations, for example in the midst of flames. You remember the torches in Nero's gardens, each torch a martyr wrapped in burning pitch as the tyrant rode past in his chariot. Others were put on ice and frozen to death, singing to their latest breath. Blandina was tossed by a wild cow, dragged away half-dead and found to be in ecstasy, worshipping the Lord. It's not natural, it's not human. And people might say, 'I don't believe it.' Well, I thank God for one experience of my own in early days preaching the gospel, antagonizing the police, being arrested, taken in, beaten up, thrown on the floor of the cell. I had an opportunity either to go into God or to resist at a human level, and I went into God. Christ came to me, and as I was beaten and punched, lying there on that floor, I suppose in a sense I went out of the body and watched what men were doing to my body, and it didn't mean a thing. There was no sensation of pain. Not until feeling returned days later was I aware of some of the parts that had been beaten. God was there.

After the beating the devil came, and he spoke to me as he had never spoken before, nor has he since.

He said, 'Suppose at the end of the day it's Satan who wins and not Christ, and it's the Christians who will be in an eternal hell, and not the followers of Satan? What then?'

In a way that I cannot explain, the temptation to be disloyal to Christ was a very real and powerful thing. But do you know that from my deepest soul there rose the answer, the choice was made deep and clear:

'If following Christ means going to hell forever, I choose hell. I choose Christ. For me, where Christ is, Heaven is, and to be without Him is hell.'

That was the deep choice of my spirit, and it has never changed: a fundamental choice, a life-choice. 'Jesus Christ for evermore.' Satan departed from me, and he never came back on any such issue.[4]

God and our Vocal Cords

There is another matter related to Wesley and the early Methodists that people reading might hardly believe. People used to ring the church bells to silence these preachers. You say, 'Look, that's a bit of nonsense. You don't need to have a great cacophony of sound to silence a solitary preacher.' Indeed, with some of the preachers who are wandering around these days you sure don't! But I tell you, if you get a Holy Ghost preacher, that can be quite another matter.

You say, 'What do you mean by that?'

I mean that the power of the Holy Spirit, the power of the mighty God, can so come upon an anointed servant that vocal cords are changed. I have experienced it hundreds of times in open-air meetings, when the voice became like the sound of a trumpet and could be heard for a great distance. The anointing of God used to fall upon us. I remember one night when Communists disputed our preaching pitch. They had arrived before our time of gathering on a Sunday night. There they were rigged up with a loudspeaker, blasting away. I suggested that we could share the time on the site.

'Oh, no,' their spokesman said, 'it's all right. We don't mind you going on as well. Just you go ahead as well.' It was fine for him. He had the loudspeaker and we hadn't.

I said, 'All right.' So we took our stance about ten or fifteen yards away — certainly not too far — and began. The anointing came, the power came, the volume came, and the communist audience came. The crowd gathered around us, and the opposition packed up what by then seemed trumpery equipment and went home.

It happens right now in the twentieth century. I totally understand the ringing of the church bells in Wesley's day, and I have no doubt that the preachers won the battle. You have no idea of the miracle that God can work.

In my own experience, one of the most amazing instances of this kind was at the funeral of the late Mr Robert Gault.[5] My voice had been strained and was badly defective. It was an open-air service, and a great number had gathered. I had a living word in my heart, but no voice to proclaim it. Just at that time I was writing a book in which I had been referring to David Wilkerson and the miracle that happened one night when the gangs were gathered, and Wilkerson came to the end of his tether. God can be very disconcerting at times. It was as though He said to me, 'What about you now? You need a miracle. You need a miracle now.' You know, by the grace of God I agreed. I opened myself to God. I believed God. And He worked a miracle. My voice became as the voice of a trumpet sounding across that whole crowd of people. God was there in power. I think Satan did not want God's honoured servant to have that kind of victorious funeral. But God loved His servant, who had been a man of God. And God, I believe, was minded that a voice of triumph would sound. God attends to these details in life. He is interested and concerned about all of that kind of thing. Ours is a miracle-working God.

A Glorious Ending

The time of Wesley's departure drew near. He had been an organizer, and his societies were growing all over the world; they grew into the Methodist movement. Whitefield on reviewing his own work could say, 'I built with a rope of sand' (I think in the sense of failing to organize his converts as Wesley had done). Towards the end Wesley uttered his ever-memorable words: 'The best of all is, God is with us!'

I occasionally look back over the years and review our own situation. I remember the early days when there was only a handful of us. I remember the moving of God, the acquiring of our first church, the revelation, the vision, the provision of the funds, the moving out into other areas, the building of other churches. I remember the actions of God. And you know, it is often easy to look backward and say, 'These were great days,' and fail to appreciate present blessing. I do not believe in overindulging in that way of thinking. I believe we are *now* having perhaps the best times we have ever had. I believe the presence of the living God is intensifying in our midst, and I believe if I was departing tonight I would remember Wesley's words and bless God's name that He is with us now. Ours is not a manmade movement, not just a strong leadership movement, but a movement of the Spirit of God expressing Christ through the lives of those who have become deeply committed Christians. 'The best of all is, God is with us!' Wesley glanced backward, but he gazed forward. Do it that way. Glance backward for encouragement, but gaze forward to the vision of glory for motivation. Christ, like Moses, *endured as seeing Him who is invisible* (Heb 11:27), and *for the joy that was set before him endured the cross, despising shame, and hath sat down at the right hand of the throne of God* (Heb 12:2).

Notes

1 I am not suggesting that we experienced revival in Billy Graham's campaigns. What we experienced was successful evangelism — a very different thing.

2 Some readers may not be familiar with terms such as Calvinism, Arminianism, election and predestination. To define the terms accurately in brief compass is not easy, but perhaps the following will be helpful.

Calvinism (the teaching of John Calvin) emphasizes the divine action in salvation, maintaining that God elects His chosen ones. Such are *foreordained* or *predestined* to have eternal life. Ordinary humanity is regarded as totally depraved, having no ability even to respond to God.

Arminianism (the teaching of the seventeenth century Dutch theologian Arminius) emphasizes human action in salvation. Man is not viewed as so utterly depraved that he cannot respond to the divine call. The subject is more fully expanded in Appendix 2.

3 An interesting story is told of Whitefield's response to one of his people who asked him if he thought they would see Wesley in Heaven. Evidently he replied that he was doubtful, since he reckoned Wesley would be so close to Christ and the throne, and they so far away. Whitefield was a very gracious man.

4 The experience of total deliverance from a given line of temptation occurred in the same way on an outstanding night in Lewis. I had had a very bad day. I had read a dangerous book which had been critical of some aspects of Pentecost, and I was due to preach in the evening. In a terrible hour waves came over me and with each wave I came nearer to drowning. There was nothing I could do to stop their coming. With every wave of dark assault I went further and further down. A point was reached when I sensed extreme danger. I feared that I would go down irrevocably. The wave came and I went down suddenly to find that 'underneath were the everlasting arms'. Christ was there: I was rescued and life returned.

At this time there was strong opposition to Pentecostal doctrine in the area (these were early, pre-Charismatic days). A meeting was coming on apace, and suddenly as I pondered,

I realized I was going to be alone; I was very much alone in Lewis. It was as though the opposition was there ringed all around, and I felt my loneliness.

'These tongues people, *tongues* people' — there was contempt for the tongues people. This present generation knows little about some of the attitudes encountered then. In these early days there was real conflict, and there I was in the midst of it.

Suddenly it struck me, if Paul were coming to the meeting that night he would be a tongues man too, and I felt a little better — indeed I felt a lot better. I didn't mind having Paul on my side. Then revelation came bit by bit. If Peter and James and John were coming, they would all be tongues people too. I felt much encouraged. If all the apostles were there, they would be tongues people too. They would all be over on my side of the room. Space was beginning to get tight! And it got really tight when it occurred to me that if most of the New Testament church could be there, they would be tongues people too.

I went out with the power and the glory on my soul, viewing in proper perspective the people who didn't believe in tongues. What an abnormal, ridiculous position for any twentieth century Christian to be in! I told them what had been revealed to me, and I hope I did it reasonably graciously. God was there. Never again did Satan come back to me on anything like that, not through all my life. The New Testament church was a Pentecostal church, the authors of the books of the New Testament were Pentecostal men, and they were writing to Pentecostal people. (I use the word Pentecostal in no narrow denominational sense. The power of Pentecost is the birthright of the whole church.) When Paul came on an abnormality such as he encountered with the Ephesian twelve (Acts 19), he set about putting it right immediately — and before many minutes they were Pentecostal too. He did not leave them in a halfway house. A great part of the evangelical church are in that halfway house now, and we have a call and a duty to present Christ and the doctrine of Pentecost in such an attractive way that they will be drawn to Him. Now I know they may be put off if we are over-aggressive or controversial.

We have to be careful about that. But they will not be put off by His magnetism when He is properly presented.

5 See the author's *Reflections on the Gifts of the Spirit* (New Dawn Books, 1988), pp. 100–1.

5 | THE WELSH REVIVAL OF 1904

I am moving on past the Great Awakening of 1859. Although it had profound results in this country, I am not minded to go into this at present, but to come up quickly to the Welsh revival of 1904.

Wales was in a very bad condition, even if not as morally low as was England in Wesley's day. In Wesley's day the churches were cold and formal; in Wales at the beginning of the twentieth century they were modernistic, having been badly affected by liberal theology. And, as so often happens, God put His hand on a man.[1] Revival often starts with God putting His hand on a man, or a woman, or a small group, drawing them into a place of deep intimacy and union with Himself. After they are affected, there is a move outward. The most holy — not the least holy — are the first convicted. In Wales God put His hand on a young man, Evan Roberts. For about six months He took that young man more or less into Heaven for four hours every night, from one o'clock to five in the morning. He was out of the body in the presence of God. He was being tuned, he was being prepared for what was to come. Then in God's time he began to preach.

The Four Principles

There were four distinctive things that Evan Roberts brought to his audiences. He looked for immediate action, and he felt that God had in vision promised him a hundred thousand souls. I want to bring to you these four things. Before presenting them, he asked the question of everyone present in his meetings: 'Do you desire an outpouring of the Spirit?' If yes, the four conditions must be met.[2] (We too shall face these four conditions and come to a place not merely of academic interest but of positive action.)

1. *Is there any sin in your past that you have not confessed to God? On your knees at once. Your past must be put away and yourself cleansed.*

Now I ask you that too. Are you carrying any known, unconfessed sin? Then stop trifling with God. There is no future for you until sin is dealt with.

2. *Is there anything in your life that is doubtful? Have you forgiven everybody, everybody, EVERYBODY? If not, don't expect forgiveness for your own sins. You won't get it.*

I ask you that same question.

3. *Do what the Spirit prompts you to do. Obedience — prompt, implicit, unquestioning obedience to the Spirit.*

Do what God tells you. I warned you about some of the danger of a misapplication of Finney's teaching, digging like a terrier to find sins that are long forgiven; don't do that. But whatever the Spirit indicates to you, do that. He makes no mistakes. If He brings up something that you have hidden for years, don't hide it any longer. Do it! Obey the Spirit, and you will find release. And you may find that He will bring another thing before you, and another, and another. He will wipe the slate clean: trust the Holy Spirit. But obey Him implicitly.

4. *A public confession of Christ as your Saviour. There is a vast difference between mere profession and real confession.*

Church membership may be nothing more than mere profession. There should be open and true confession to a relationship with the living Lord.

The Reaping

They went down like corn before the reaper, as the Holy
Spirit swept large areas of Wales, north and south. And
oh, the power and the glory of it, the miners saved in
masses, wrongs righted, deep sins forgiven, magistrates
with no cases to judge, pubs emptied, football terraces
emptied, various halls of iniquity emptied, and the voice
of swearing no longer heard on many of the streets: men
were afraid to swear, so intense was the power. The jour-
nalists smelled a story, and they came and heard the voice
of the living God, and were converted where they sat. The
power of God was there, and souls came in masses. There
was an outpouring of glory. And Evan Roberts got his
hundred thousand souls.

Social Consequences

Let us look for a moment at the outcome of the revival
socially.

The newspapers reported that since the commencement of
the revival there had been very few arrests for drunkenness.
In Rhos, a North Wales mining town, the justices of the peace
were presented with white gloves, signifying that there were
no cases for trial. The official police records show that in
Glamorgan in 1903 there were 10,528 convictions for drunkenness. In 1906 these figures had decreased [by almost half].
As a result of this there was a great improvement in moral
standards. The public houses and gambling dens now lay
empty, theatres closed, and the terraces at football grounds
were empty and desolate. As the hardened unbelievers were
gloriously converted, confessions of awful sins were heard
on every side. Bad debts from many years previous were paid
back with interest. The revival affected the Welsh miners
more than any of these men. They were transformed in an
instant. They would be seen praying with each other before
starting in the coalmine. The pit ponies, who lived in an
awful environment, subject to brutality and cruelty at the
hands of the hauliers, only being accustomed to commands

with foul language, were now totally confused and almost stopped working until they became adjusted to the new kindness and clean language.

Family situations were changed. Men now spent time with their children instead of drinking; cruelty to children also decreased, and the number of prosecutions for child cruelty fell to almost nothing in the county of Glamorgan.[3]

Worldwide Effects

Finally, the streams and the influence of that revival went worldwide. Communication had become much easier in the twentieth century than in earlier days. News of the Welsh revival flashed across the world, and its influence went into many lands. What some of you don't know is that its influence is with us now. Our background sources, the springs from which our own fellowships come, are of two types, and one of these is Welsh. The 1904 revival had a profound influence on the Jeffreys brothers, and it was George Jeffreys who brought a knowledge of Pentecost to Greenock. It was under his preaching that Miss Taylor, a founder of our movement, was convicted of sin. She was powerfully converted, and there was always in her spirit a known affinity with that earlier movement in Wales. Through her the influence of the Welsh revival is alive in many of your hearts, although you have not necessarily been aware of where the life-stream came from. It is nevertheless one part of your heritage.

> PRAYER: *It is too easy to recall how wonderfully God moved in Wales, and forget the background, forget the dealing with sin, forget the searching of the Holy Spirit. But, Lord, what is the point in our endlessly looking at yesterdays, when we shall be judged in relation to today? There is a sense in which there is no tomorrow. There is a sense in which we only have today in which to act. Tomorrow may never come for those who are putting off decision. Lord, we ask for decision now — a yielding to You of any unconfessed*

sin of the past, any unforgiveness in the heart…. We
pray that You will be glorified. We are not looking, O
Lord, for merely emotional responses, but for a
clearing away of the burden of sin, the cleansing by
the blood of the Lord Jesus, not just on the surface, but
deep down.

Ponder it; realize that God never teases His people. He doesn't hold out a plate and then refuse food. He doesn't hold out a cup and remove it before we put it to our lips. When he holds out a cup He asks us to drink it. When He supplies food He asks us to eat it. He has supplied food now, and has given opportunity. He has shown the door of entrance which is through Christ Jesus, who came 'to seek and to save that which is lost', to give life and to give it abundantly, to give release, to give pardon, to make us new creatures and to lead us on in a new life, putting on the Lord Jesus.

Let your faith rise, and believe God, that the thing that you have sought is yours. Have faith in God. Without faith it is impossible to please God. But you have a strong ground, a strong foundation for your faith in the Word of God. *Come unto Me, all ye that labour and are heavy laden, and I will give you rest* (Mat 11:28). *I came that they may have life, and may have it abundantly* (Jn 10:10). The gates of Heaven are open, the place of reconciliation is there at the cross of Jesus. Make it yours now in the deeps of your deep heart, for Christ's sake.

Notes

[1] This is not to suggest that Evan Roberts was God's sole instrument. Indeed, there was a movement of the Spirit in Wales for some time prior to 1904.
[2] This and the succeeding material in italics is taken from Colin Whittaker, *Great Revivals* (Marshall, Morgan & Scott, 1984), p. 92.

³ I am indebted to Duncan Allan K. Wiggins for this quotation (slightly adapted) from his unpublished essay, 'The History of the Welsh Revival 1904'. The statistics for Glamorgan are culled from J. Vyrnwy Morgan, *The Welsh Religious Revival, 1904–05: A Retrospect and a Criticism* (Chapman & Hall, 1909), p. 247.

6 | THE LEWIS REVIVAL

I am aware as I speak of the Lewis revival that much about it has already been heard over the years. With various incidents you may be familiar, but I imagine that there is still much in the background that most people really know little or nothing about. I want to approach the subject from a personal point of view, and give you personal reflections about things that I know, some of which I heard from the lips of Mr Campbell himself. Other matters I have learned at second hand, and I want to distinguish between the two categories. You may find that there is much to interest you.[1]

To go back to the earliest stages, in my university days I met a young student who had been converted under Mr Campbell when he was a minister of the United Free Church in Falkirk. At an earlier time Mr Campbell had worked with the Faith Mission, and evidently he felt a call to return to work with them.

It was probably from the same student that I learned how there came a night in Mr Campbell's life when he was in prayer and became greatly concerned about the youth of the Hebrides. There seemed to come on him a tremendous burden, and he saw the youth of that area going into hell. There was nothing wishy-washy about his views on this kind of thing. He believed in a hell from which he felt he had a duty to warn all to flee. He seems to have had an exceptional vision that night, and there came upon him a deep call and a deep urge to go and give warning.[2] He had a mission in Skye before going on to Lewis, and there were early manifestations of the miraculous and phenomenal in Skye. Evidently he was bitterly opposed, and was accused of hypnotizing his audiences, for example. I understand that one of his main opponents dropped dead in rather unusual circumstances, and I gather that something of the fear of God came as a result. Some regarded this as divine intervention. That part of his life and work I cannot go into with verifiable detail.[3]

A Personal Interlude

But I come to a part with which I am better acquainted. Much of what follows I heard from Mr Campbell's own lips. But prior to hearing about the revival itself, there was one very interesting and remarkable occurrence. I met him by design; I wanted to hear about the revival. And I want you to note this, because it has a bearing on what revival is like. As he began to tell me about events in Lewis and to quote Scripture that had been used on one occasion when revival broke out, suddenly I felt that he almost disappeared and I became aware of an area of my life about which God was displeased. The word was extremely strong and condemning: *But after thy hardness and impenitent heart treasurest up for thyself wrath in the day of wrath and revelation of the righteous judgement of God* (Rom 2:5). I became almost unconscious as the power of revival came crashing into my life. Mr Campbell continued to speak, and I continued to feel the operation of the power of God in terrible strength.

Let me tell you this: you may be pursuing a way of life with which you are comparatively happy; you may not even know clearly that you are in error or in sin, or you may have a gentle idea that all may not be well. But when revival comes, God does not ask you to consider the matter. He does not take you out on an intellectual flight of imagination. You don't sit down and weigh things up and wonder. He comes in an absolute sense and He dictates. You are not asked for your opinion: you are given

His judgment. And you may not alter it. You may not change it. It is absolute; it is authoritative; some might call it dictatorial: so different from what our modern generation like to think about considered opinions and weighing matters up, looking at pros and cons, and giving intellectual judgments. There is a time for these things, but not when God comes in revival. Then we are under the sound of the voice of the living God, and we know that voice is not the voice of a man. We accept it, or we reject it at our eternal peril. The experience shook me to my foundations. I knew the intervention of God.

I remember speaking to Miss Taylor not long after I had met Mr Campbell, and she had quite a remarkable experience. I'll never forget this. She suddenly seemed to look into the far distances, if I might put it that way, and she said: 'That man's life and yours are intertwined. You will meet again. There is a strange connection.' (I can't remember the exact words, but they were to that effect.) Miss Taylor was not only a prophetess; she was a seer. She saw events that were still future. Mr Campbell's life and mine did intertwine, as some of my previous books have shown, and the nature of the connection will emerge as we consider the Lewis revival now. It was a strange intertwining indeed.

What Revival Is

As I have said, Mr Campbell told me part of the story of Lewis with his own lips. He said, 'Revival is neither more nor less than the impact of the personality of Jesus Christ upon a life or upon a community.' He indicated that when He comes in this way on a community, the place becomes God-conscious. Not just the best people in the church, not just the church alone, but the whole community is affected. Revival affects the atmosphere on the streets. It affects people who had previously little knowledge or interest in God or the things of God. Suddenly they become God-conscious.

That is of vital significance. That is why I rejoice so much now on Saturday nights as people who gather from many parts become deeply God-conscious. It is the beginning of revival when people become God-conscious. Not particularly conscious of men or choirs or song-leaders or praise teams. There is a consciousness of the living God, and as people are caught up into that consciousness and God dictates His terms, revival is on the way. God-consciousness: 'the impact of the personality of Christ upon a life or a community'.

One of the first things that comes with the impact of the personality of Christ is conviction of sin on every life that is not right with God. God does not come in power and leave you unaffected. The dark things come welling up, the hurts, the pains, the grievances, the hatreds, the jealousies, the things of the flesh. You face your lust, your unbrokenness. In the searching light of God your sins are uncovered, they are revealed. You cannot stand in that presence and hold them. When God comes in power, He comes as a consuming fire, and He burns up the dross of life. *It is a fearful thing to fall into the hands of the living God* (Heb 10:31), for, as Paul said, *our God is a consuming fire* (12:29). On the other hand, it is a wonderful thing to fall into the hands of God, for it is also true that our God is full of compassion and love and tenderness, and He heals the hearts of men. He sets the prisoners free, and He gives light to those who sit in darkness. He meets us in whatever condition He finds us, if we but bow the knee. He has a total answer for human need.

An Unusual Invitation

Mr Campbell began to tell me some of the detail of his first going to Lewis. He had received an invitation from a Church of Scotland minister, the Rev James MacKay of the parish of Barvas. Mr Campbell had previously preached at a national convention at Strathpeffer, and two old ladies of Barvas, though never having heard or met him, encouraged their minister to invite Mr Campbell because God was minded to visit them with revival, and Mr Campbell was God's chosen instrument. Mr Campbell, however, declined the invitation because of a previous engagement. The old ladies, nothing daunted, were convinced that Mr Campbell was the man God wanted there, that the invitation and the timing was in God's will, and that in fact he would be there. In his reply Mr Campbell wrote that if for any reason his previous engagement fell through, he would come.

Meeting Peggy and Christine Smith

The engagement did fall through, and the hour came when he found himself on Lewis and in the presence of these two ladies. They were both aged; the older of the two was eighty-four and was, I think, in bed when Mr Campbell arrived. I often refer to this, but for the sake of those to whom it is new, I will go over the story. It bears repeating.

Peggy looked at him, and said, 'Yes, you're God's man after all.'

'But', he said, 'you don't know me. We've never met.'

'Oh, yes,' she said, 'I know you,' and she proceeded to tell him that on a certain day, at a certain hour in the day, the devil had tried to kill him, but at that hour, she said, 'The precious blood of Jesus came between you and him, and you were saved' (from natural death).

I think he had a fearful shock. He told me that at that hour on that day he was on his motorbike between Falkirk and Edinburgh. A Rover car travelling at speed came out of a side road, skimmed past him, and landed over the hedge with everybody in it. Mr Campbell was almost wiped away, and a bus driver who had almost been involved in the accident came out of his cab in great consternation, reckoning that a miracle had occurred. I think he felt that something supernatural had happened to his steering wheel.

The old lady said, 'The devil tried to kill you, but at two o'clock in the afternoon the precious blood of Jesus came between you and him, and you were saved.'

Mr Campbell went on to tell me that as he got to know these two old ladies he realized that there was a dimension of spiritual life of which he had no previous knowledge. They enjoyed a relationship with Christ that he had not experienced, and they had an intimacy with Christ which was new to him. He found in them a power in prayer that was phenomenal. They would pray thus: 'Lord, You promised to give me ten souls today and, Lord, if You will not do it, how will I ever be able to trust You again?' That was not presumptuous prayer, he said, but a prayer of real faith: it betokened a relationship with God where they had heard the voice of God and leaned all their weight upon what He said, believing it absolutely as Abraham believed God. You can understand that they felt they would be shattered if the promise was not fulfilled; they did not for a moment believe that such a thing could happen. The wording of their prayer expressed the strength of their claiming of the promise given, and of their grip in faith until they saw it fulfilled.

He cited one particular example from the revival itself. Normally there was a fierce contest with hell before revival broke out in a community. Then came the blazing power of God, and people were deeply affected. Knowledge of events would then spread into neighbouring parts of the Island. There would be various reactions. It wasn't everybody who was holding out their hands and calling on God for revival. There was a particular village which up to that time had been unaffected, and was in fact opposed to the revival. Peggy, the older lady, told Mr Campbell on this occasion to go to that village. But he was not minded to do any such thing and objected that he had not been invited, and that the people there were opposed to the revival. That had no effect on the old lady. She had heard from Heaven. And I tell you this. When you find a stalwart who has heard from Heaven, there is no point in arguing. It gets you absolutely nowhere. There was no point at all in his arguing.

So he did what so many of us do when the voice of God sounds. Instead of obeying it, he said, 'Well, we'll pray about it.' Prayer is often the last resort of the disobedient. Yes, I mean that: please remember it. When you get an order from God, He doesn't ask you to pray about it; He asks you to obey it. When Montgomery gave an order to the Eighth Army in El Alamein days, he didn't expect the troops to pray about it or discuss it; he expected the troops to jump to it and do what they were told.

His orders, I seem to remember him saying, were not given to form a basis for discussion. When God tells you to do something, don't use prayer as a means of arguing with God. Just do it.

The time came when they prayed. I presume he went down on his knees, and I don't know whether he got to the point of praying or not, but *she* prayed. (She had obviously no inhibitions about women praying or giving instruction to a man either, even to one of the most greatly used men of God in Britain in that day. She had no inhibitions as a woman in telling him what to do. Just be remembering that, any of you who are unduly prejudiced against women ministry! She, the woman, instructed him.[4]) Thus she prayed: 'Lord, I have given this man the message You gave me, but he doesn't appear to be willing to obey it. Lord, give this man wisdom.' I picture him rising and scratching his head a bit and saying,

'Well, I suppose I better go.'

'Yes,' she said, 'you better go. And you'll not be preaching for fifteen minutes until the Lord will give you seven souls.' Not six, not eight, but seven. Fifteen minutes. No meeting arranged, no invitation. And away he went — maybe rather reluctantly.

A Strange Phenomenon

The next part you may find difficult to believe. I do not, because having been in Lewis I have known this kind of thing operate. There can come a consciousness upon an individual or a group suddenly to do something. It may come on people all at the same time, and it seems to have happened in this case. When Mr Campbell arrived in the village, there was a house choc-a-bloc full of people waiting for his coming. In the event he couldn't get in, and had to preach from the outside.

He had not been preaching for fifteen minutes before an elder made his way out and said, 'You'll have to stop preaching. You'll have to get in here.' They made a way for him and he squeezed in, and there he found lying in an inner room prostrate bodies. He counted them: one, two, three, four, five, six, *seven*. And they all eventually rose truly born again.[5]

A depth of relationship with God. An inner knowledge of what the Lord was doing. *The secret of the LORD is with them that fear Him* (Ps 25:14), and these ladies lived in that dimension.

Outbreak in Barvas

Now to tell you that incident I have jumped forward a little. The revival broke out in the parish to which Mr Campbell was first invited, Barvas, an area I know well. There was a small praying group, some of whom had been involved in the '39 revival. Mr Campbell had preached on the first night, and nothing in particular had happened. This group then invited him to an all-night prayer meeting. It was a remarkable meeting. God seems to have impressed them with the verses, *Who shall ascend into the hill of the* LORD*? And who shall stand in his holy place? He that hath clean hands, and a pure heart; Who hath not lifted up his soul unto vanity, And hath not sworn deceitfully* (Ps 24:3–4). The young deacon who brought this word challenged the company: 'Are our hands clean? Is the heart pure?' There had to be a getting right with God, to have a life with no shadows. There must be no barriers between the soul and God. There came a moment sometime before morning when they knew they had broken through to God, and that revival would come.

Came the night: the church was full, and the service came to an end. Nothing particularly phenomenal had happened by that point. Then a young man who had remained in the church after most others had dispersed prayed fervently and went prostrate in a trance-like condition. His piercing cry arrested the attention of many who had lingered in the churchyard, and they poured back into the church. Something phenomenal then occurred. The presence of God intensified, bringing conviction of sin and repentance. People were powerfully affected. The movement spread beyond the church to many who had gathered outside. There they knelt beside the boulders of the churchyard, getting right with God as the mighty power of God swept over them. Revival was born that night.

Typical Revival Scenes

I want to give you a typical scene as I have heard Mr Campbell explain it. He might be preaching and know that God was there but had not broken through in power. He might halt the service and call on a person known to be powerful in prayer to rise and intercede. Either then or during the preaching the break might come. He said there would come a point when it was like the bursting of a bomb in the midst of them. Suddenly the Holy Spirit would sweep down in power, and there would be a shattering spiritual explosion. People would be affected all over the congregation. There could be and frequently were physical manifestations, there could be prostrations, with God moving from heart to heart and seat to seat. He said that when the explosion came he stopped preaching and sat down. The Holy Spirit moved, and revival fire burned.

I can give you one example of this kind of scene. He had been preaching in a church which I well know, having preached in it myself in Lewis. I don't want to name it, because if I mention names too closely people may identify individuals, and that is not always a wise thing to have happen. In this particular church the going was very hard. The meetings were being held in typical Highland fashion. Now this is something of which many of you may have no knowledge. Some of you may pray at greater length than is wise, but you are unlikely to compare with some of our Highland brethren. A public prayer might go on for a solid half-hour. Imagine four of the elders praying at that length at the beginning of a meeting. Two hours of solid prayer. I think Mr Campbell put up with this for a night or two, and then probably felt that revival would never break out if it continued. He arrived at the meeting on the next night, and asked to speak to the elders before the meeting began. He said, as best I remember, 'I always understood that the men of _____ [naming the church] were godly men, and men of prayer. Now in my opinion a godly man, a man of prayer, is a man who spends so long with God in prayer in his own home that he has almost nothing left to say when he comes to the house of God. That is my definition of a godly man.' The prayers after that were remarkably short. And revival broke out.

One of Mr Campbell's friends was Coinneach Beag. This was a real man of God, a man of prayer and a visionary. Coinneach became aware that God was going to move in a particular church, and told Mr Campbell this. They went over and Mr Campbell began to preach and again encountered difficulty. There came a point in one service when he stopped preaching and asked Coinneach to pray. Now I want you to understand this. I recollect that when another Lewis man, Norman Campbell, was powerfully used in prayer, I could feel the effect and actually see the darkness in the spiritual world recede. I want you to understand the reality and effectiveness of a certain type of prayer. Duncan Campbell called on Coinneach Beag. And Coinneach got up and laid hold on God. And that is a very different matter from uttering long prayers that do not have God's anointing on them. Mr Campbell told me that he opened his eyes at one point and saw Coinneach standing there with his two fists up like a boxer as he prayed. Then Coinneach used remarkable language. He said, 'Please excuse me one moment, Lord, while I address the devil.' This he then did with great force, and the bomb exploded. Revival fell on that church that night.

Mr Campbell said, 'The next I saw of Coinneach, he was stretched out on one of the benches sound asleep.' He had done his work, he had fulfilled what God wanted him to do; it was for others to do their part as Coinneach slept.

I want to speak further of that phenomenal thing — the gathering of a company supernaturally. I can't explain this easily to a southern audience; you need to feel it, you need to sense it. There is a new word that has been coming into vogue amongst us recently, bad usage though it may be: *feel to*, corrupted to *feelty* (or *feel tae*). In revival time sometimes not just one or two people, but a whole company, would 'feel to' come. They would then gather together. Evidently on the small island of Bernera on the west coast of Lewis, there came a point when everybody turned and went to church — whether people were going shopping, or cutting peat, or whatever. Some were out on the water fishing at the time, but they too came together. God met them in power, and I think that all, or almost all, of the unconverted in that community turned to Christ.

Demons and Angels Both Visible

There was another incident that I found remarkable, which I think you will not find in any of the books so far published about the Lewis revival; Mr Campbell did not broadcast it. He was not moving in Pentecostal circles generally, where it would have been more acceptable, I imagine, than in certain other evangelical circles. He told of one district where he had gone. There was a prayer meeting in progress before the time came to preach. I have the impression that the Christians had gathered in a kind of tin hut. I don't know the detail, nor indeed do I know the place, but the information I do have came from Mr Campbell directly to me. As the people prayed, there came a breakthrough. Now mark this. He said, 'I opened my eyes, and I saw the demons fly in all directions.' The power of God came and the demons could not remain in the hour of the power of God. The demons had been present in numbers in that hall. Note: this was not a company of occultists; it was not a company of devil-worshippers; it was not a witchcraft circle. This was a company of possibly the choicest men and women of God in that area. 'The demons fled in all directions.' I am not for a moment suggesting that these people had been demon-possessed. But I am more than suggesting that the demons were giving tremendous attention to these people. They would possibly be tempting them, they would be tormenting them, they would be around them, trying to influence them, they would be opposing their prayers. It is possible, of course, that some demons may have been inside particular individuals. But whether in or out, when the power of God came there certainly was a great scattering. His servant saw them flee in all directions.

Were that power coming to you now in that degree, do you realize that you could not easily endure the continued presence of a demon, even although it was associated with a favourite lust or hidden desire? You could not live with it; you would have to come to terms with God or turn aside. In the Lewis case the demons fled the divine presence. Mr Campbell went on to tell me that the praying company went out of the hut and found that people were coming from all over the community, some carrying benches, preparing for an open-air service. He said, 'The power of God fell, and great big men went down prostrate.' Some were evidently deep sinners. Every man amongst them, I believe, was totally saved. The power was divine: wonderful, glorious.

God can do more in 'one divine moment' than man could do in a thousand lifetimes. Learn to depend on God, to look for the action of God, to trust God. In the hour of the release of His power, when there comes flooding down the very life of God, you will literally find that He will do more in seconds of time than you could ever do. Such is the action of the living God: He searches His church to the utmost, He heals, He empowers, He changes lives. He changes churches and communities.

And oh, the changes that came to these Highland places. In some areas it meant the ending of drunkenness and the closing of the drinking houses. Lives were deeply changed, and the sound of the songs of Zion rang out wonderfully. Spiritual song rose gloriously. Gaelic can sometimes seem 'dreich' to southern ears, but it can also be glorious, when it is under the anointing of the Holy Spirit. There they sang, and there at times they evidently heard the heavenly choirs under an open heaven. Angels were seen. Once a man told his friend that revival would break out in a particular village that night.

'How do you know?' his friend asked.

'Because I saw the angels going over this afternoon.'

The incoming of another dimension, a realm in the Spirit, a wonderful place, a wonderful life.

And What of the Message?

The message of revival was fearful, awesome, glorious. I usually illustrate the fearful aspect by quoting the old Highland lady referred to earlier. A Bible-lover, a Bible-believer, having no difficulties with the doctrine of hell, under no wrong influence of ultimate reconciliation or annihilation teaching, she believed in the hell of the Bible. But when she heard the preaching of a man anointed with power for the hour, she said in her Gaelic way: 'The hell of the Bible is terrible. But oh, the hell of Duncan Campbell!' It was as though the hell of the Bible was recognized and people could think about it objectively, but the hell of Duncan Campbell came surging up as he preached and the fire of it was all around. The fear of the living God came down.

I remember in my own case being carried or carrying someone into hell in a dream in my early days. The horror of it never left my life: hell. If I am preaching to an audience favourably disposed and open to the message of God, I find that I can touch a particular depth on this theme. If I am preaching to a more materialistic audience that is much further away from spiritual things, I may find that I cannot touch the same level, and I have to be careful not to give what is inappropriate. You who have ears to hear, hear what is said of hell.

Yes, the message in the Lewis revival was fearful, awesome and effective. The great fundamental facts were emphasized — human depravity and man's utter inability to save himself, the judgment of God on sin in all its forms, the reality of hell, the atonement of Calvary and the love of God for man.

Revival brought to the surface a sense of the severity of

God that was startling, and (as I indicated earlier) when the way opened for Mr Campbell to preach in Stornoway he wondered if his approach should be modified. I imagine him sitting down and thinking things out. It is not always wise in the spiritual world to think things out. It is better to receive the authoritative direction of God. In the country parts there was a different atmosphere from that in Stornoway. The fear of God was more deeply amongst the people.

However that may be, God made it clear to Mr Campbell that the message was not to change. He preached the same message in Stornoway unvarnished, and God moved in Stornoway in power. A day came later when he was speaking of revival in England. Even then, as I have said, dangerous doctrines were rife in some evangelical circles, and the message of judgment and condemnation and eternal punishment was not always welcome. We may pray and beat our breasts for revival, but when revival comes it will be God's revival, and it will come God's way. The doctrines will be those dictated by God, and not by man, and may not conform to modern ideas as to what is reasonable. God will not change — but, my friends, our views may have to change radically. The doctrine of hell is an offensive doctrine, but blessed are men when they are not offended in God. The fact that something is offensive does not make it untrue. The doctrines that the Holy Spirit brings will not be engineered by man to fit into the prejudices of man. In revival men are turned upside down: they have no standing, no locus. Our only place is prostrate, broken before the cross of Jesus Christ.

When God called me personally and gave a particular ministry of deliverance, commissioning me to take the message of cleansing and deliverance to the church, He indicated quite clearly that the commission He had given me in an earlier day to take Pentecost to an unwilling generation often did not make me popular, and neither would the later commission. I am aware that the teaching I am giving you now would have me excluded from many a pulpit. Many who know me have become and are becoming conditioned to it, but in many places men have itching ears and heap to themselves teachers who will not disturb them by telling them the blunt truth as it is in Christ and in the Bible. Now the principles I am teaching you are not new. They are principles that run through every revival of which I have ever known, every revival that ever blazed across any part of the face of earth. What is heretical is the denial of these doctrines, sometimes these days even by leading Christians. Such heresies have surfaced from age to age. These are not the teachings of God. The teachings of God never change. The principles are eternal principles.

The Lewis revival blazed and affected the lives of many people on the Island and far beyond. It ultimately abated, and it is not my purpose to analyse the reasons for that. But the time came when the revival as it was generally known could be said to have ended. I do not mean that the spiritual life of the people affected came to an end, but that phenomenal blaze died down. My presence in Lewis coincided with that later period. Mr Campbell was having difficulty over accommodation in one of the last places in which he held a campaign in Lewis: a village called Gravir. I offered to be his chauffeur for most of a week, and I took him night by night to the meetings. They were good meetings, but not what would be described as revival meetings.

God's Plan, Not Mine

I had long been interested in revival, and for purposes unrelated to the revival God had taken me to Lewis. But the natural part of me had a notion. I had recently taken an honours degree in history, and it occurred to me that it would be good to write a history of the Lewis revival and help to take some pressure off Mr Campbell, who was under considerable fire by that time from opponents of the revival. I could gather details from Mr Campbell and go round the Island to take evidence from the people concerned. I would write as a historian and publish a book which might have been of considerable interest. Now wasn't that a great notion? But God wasn't in it, and I knew that quite sharply. God wanted me to take the message of Pentecost to Lewis, to meet the needs of the people as God made His spiritual provision for them, not just to titillate the ears of other sections of the Christian world with historical details of revival — interesting and indeed beneficial as those might have been. And now that I come to speak and write of the Lewis revival, I can shed lights on it that I might never have done at that earlier time. This is not an academic, historical account of that revival; it is an attempt to unveil spiritual truths associated with it. It touches on some issues not previously well known. There is, I trust, spiritual revelation rather than a mere historical appraisal.[6]

Again and again people who had experienced revival were later gloriously baptized in the Holy Spirit. The message with which God sent me was appropriate to their needs in that post-revival period.[7]

An Area of Difference

It would be wrong to give the impression that I was involved with Mr Campbell in revival, or that we saw eye to eye on all matters. With much of his doctrine I deeply agreed, but he was not carrying the banner of Pentecost as I knew it, and indeed I felt at times he was not a friend of the work in which I was involved.[8] I was not prepared to turn aside from my God-given task. On perhaps the last occasion when he was in my car and I told him of some recent happenings and of people who had been baptized in the Spirit, I felt in my spirit it was like a blow to him.

This is what I felt, but I am not in a position to state it categorically. But God was minded to pour out the power of Pentecost.

I give a word to those of you who have aspirations for God. If there was one man who might have turned me aside in taking the full message of Pentecost to Lewis, I cannot think of any who would have been more likely to succeed than the late Duncan Campbell, because of the way God had used him and because of my respect for him. And, you know, it didn't have the effect of the weight of a feather, because the power of the living God was operating in me. It is a strange thing, but in earlier days there was one man in Brethren circles who had a more profound effect on me than any other man in all the rest of the movement. And would you believe it: he was in the very act of writing three articles against Pentecost when I was baptized in the Spirit. My baptism happened between two of the articles. If there was one man who might have deflected me, he was that man — yet the effect that he had on me was negligible. Never allow any man or woman to influence you adversely by a hairbreadth when you have the clear call and commission of the living God. Many in Lewis were filled with the Holy Spirit, and there are ministers in the Church of Scotland today who in the aftermath of that revival were baptized in the Holy Ghost. Blessed be the name of the Lord.

> PRAYER: *Lord our God, we pray that Thou wilt imprint the lessons of revival upon us now. Prepare our hearts and minds and spirits for the visitation of the living God. Lord, draw nearer still. Let Thy power, we pray Thee, deepen in the midst of us.*

Notes

[1] Much valuable information on Duncan Campbell's life and his ministry in Lewis is contained in Andrew A. Woolsey's

Channel of Revival (The Faith Mission, 1974), with which my own account can be compared.

2 Woolsey writes:

> Immediately he seemed to be in a trance gazing into caverns of death, witnessing the agonies of hell. With horror he saw thousands from the Highlands and Islands of Scotland drifting to their doom, and heard a voice calling: 'Go to them, go to them.'
>
> Duncan always believed in the existence of hell but from that moment it was an unquestioning reality. Lost souls were really lost. He must warn them. He must tell them of God's way of escape (*Channel of Revival*, pp. 98–9).

3 For further information on Mr Campbell's experiences in Skye, see *Channel of Revival*, chap. 12.

4 To understand the scriptural justification of this, see *A Trumpet Call to Women*, especially chaps. 7 and 9.

5 Mr Woolsey's version varies very slightly in detail. See *Channel of Revival*, p. 120.

6 One strange matter of spiritual significance comes back to mind. Mr Campbell once told me of a particular battle with Satan. He said that normally Satan tries to pull a man down, but if the man is faithful God stands by him, the Bible speaks to him, and the work goes forward. Even in the midst of intense conflict the work goes on. On this occasion he said, 'The devil pushed me up the way.' Evidently he felt he entered a strange dimension. He seemed to be unaware of taking any wilful wrong step — but suddenly the Bible stopped speaking comfortingly and revival dried up. He sought God and discerned where he had gone off the track and repented. God restored him, but, he said, he had to be extremely disciplined on the issue concerned for quite some time afterwards — until, I presume, the danger was safely passed.

This is worth noting. Always be particularly careful when Satan tries to disguise himself as an angel of light. A way can seem a very happy way, a comfortable way, a spiritual way, and be quite a wrong way. Avoid ways that bypass the cross. And remember the temptation of Eden — to do something which might be thought to make Eve a better and a wiser person, to be indeed a more God-like person. Our enemy is subtle, but there are certain sure signs of his hoof-prints. The

Bible is ever a reliable guide. When it is silent or speaks to you in condemning terms, take note and obey.

7 My own experiences in Lewis are described in various of my earlier books, in particular *The Clash of Tongues: With Glimpses of Revival*. They also form the theme of two chapters in a forthcoming book of personal reminiscences related to revival.

8 For the record, I should say that I learned a few years ago that Mr Campbell himself *had* spoken in tongues. He never told me personally of this, but I know and trust the word of the minister who conveyed the information to me. He was at one time a student under Mr Campbell and questioned him closely on the issue.

PART TWO

COMING REVIVAL
The Vision of Jean Darnall

7 | THE VISION

Mr Black's Introduction

Many years ago I learned of Jean Darnall's vision of coming revival in Scotland. I felt an immediate witness to it, and indeed in our own fellowship we believed that revival was coming. When in 1987 we heard of the vision from her own lips there was a very deep response. The occasion was in the City Halls in Glasgow before a large audience. Many were effectively ministered to in that meeting.

Before Jean left Britain to return to the United States in 1992, I was one of the speakers who paid public tribute to her in a farewell meeting in Larbert. After that meeting I suggested that she should put the full detail of her vision in a book, and if not, that she might allow me to do it.[1]

She later wrote me a very gracious letter giving me full permission to use anything she had said that might be useful. Accordingly in this book on revival I am delighted to incorporate her vision. It is hoped that its retelling here will kindle desire and prayer in many hearts for its fulfilment.

Jean's ministry is very gentle and gracious, and she has a very keen sense of humour. I remember she started her address in Glasgow with what some serious citizens might have felt was somewhat inappropriate but I thought very funny. It certainly put her audience at ease, and no doubt warmed their hearts. I quote her:

> I heard of a meeting at the Royal Albert Hall where someone had been preaching for about an hour and three-quarters. It

had been rather in a monotone and very difficult to hear. However, someone from the back row in one of the balconies shouted out, 'We can't hear!' and before the speaker could say anything, someone on the front row stood up and said, 'Thank God and sit down!'

Jean Darnall Tells her Story

The Lord told me when He sent me up to Scotland that I wasn't to plan any sort of itinerary, except that I could have a starting-off point. A significant letter arrived just at the time when I was praying about that starting-off point. 'Where do You want me to go first, Lord, in order to begin this special mission?' — and there was this letter from the Greenock Methodist pastor. So the Methodists welcomed me, and we had a tremendous time on the first day in their newly decorated sanctuary. Many visitors came, the blessing came down, people came to the Lord, and some were healed. It was an unforgettable day.

The Lord had said, 'If you do this — if you will go without a planned itinerary — then you will meet lots of people whom I want you to meet whom you don't know at all. And you'll go to places that you know nothing about.'

And I certainly have done that. I have met thousands of people in these last five weeks, all over Scotland, and I have been to places whose names I cannot pronounce even yet. When people ask me where I've been, I get my diary out and say, 'There: that's where I was.' I think when I finish in Kelso tomorrow evening, I will have ministered in about fifty-two places in these five weeks, besides many in-between stops, just meeting individuals. And I feel like I must be a sister to Barnabas. You know, he was the son of encouragement, and I think I've been a sister of encouragement. It seems like that's been my main ministry. Well, we can stand a lot of encouragement!

En Route for Hongkong

I sound as if I had just arrived in this country. But many of you know that my husband and I live in London.

Someone said, 'How come you live in London?'

I said, 'Well, a funny thing happened to me on the way to Hongkong.'

My husband was in Hongkong twenty-one years ago. He was there on a short-term project of organizing a high school for Chinese refugee children who had come up through the missionary schools. When those children in Kowloon came to high school age, they would go into communist-run high schools, and many of the young people were being lost. My husband saw the need of organizing a high school, but the missionaries were so busy with all their other activities they couldn't get it done. So he went back to dedicate himself to that special job, and he had been gone a year.

In the meantime the Lord had spoken to me in the United States. He gave me the scripture: *Go sell all that you have and give it away to the poor, and come and follow me, and in this world you'll have reward, and in the world to come* and so forth. I contacted my husband and shared the word with him and asked him what to do. But I didn't want him to get too worried. He was way over there in Hongkong living Chinese-style in one room with a couple of pet rats (he said). I thought he must really be looking forward to coming back to his home, and he wouldn't want to come back and find out that I had sold it, you know, while he was away. So I tucked this scripture in the middle of the letter and I said, 'By the way, there's a scripture keeps going over my mind, all the time, about selling everything, giving it away to the poor, and so on. I've tried to get a sermon on it, but it won't gel. What do you think?'

And he sent back a letter tape and said, 'You know exactly what that scripture means. And the Lord has already spoken to me — before I left for Hongkong. So go ahead.'

So the Lord had lightened our load considerably: He had done a lot of pruning and cutting back.

When I came to England, it was the first part of what I thought would be a trip around the world. The Lord had said, 'I want you to go to Europe,' and I thought that meant Hongkong. Now I know my geography better than that, but I thought that it meant that Europe was my first stop on my way to Hongkong. However, when I arrived here and ministered for the Fountain Trust movement with Michael Harper, my daughter and I went on then to the Continent and were intending to continue the itinerary. But when I was in Hanover, Michael contacted me again and asked me if I'd come back to England.

I wrote back to him, 'Thank you, Michael, for the invitation. But I nearly froze to death in October in England, and I don't relish the idea of coming back in January. Please invite me in the summer some time! I never saw a country with so many chimneys and so little fire!'

I have to admit I didn't even pray too much about it, because I was just sure the Lord loved me more than that, you know!

Call to England

But during the night, as we were sleeping between those big down feather ticks that they have in Germany, my daughter La Donna shook me and woke me up. This didn't happen to her very often — in fact I don't know if it ever happened before or since. She said, 'Mum, the Lord just woke me up and He told me that we're to go back to England and stay there for as long as He has need of us.'

I said, 'Roll over: you're having a bad dream!'

But in the morning we prayed about it together, and I realized that she and the Lord were on the same side. So, although a couple of weeks had gone by, I called Michael and said, 'Do you still want me?' and he said, 'Oh, yes. Corrie Ten Boom was supposed to come, but she's had a car accident, and I really would like to have a lady here representing the ladies at the conference.' So we changed our plans, and I cancelled the trip to Italy, from where I was going on to the Middle East. I cancelled just enough to give me time to go to England. And when we arrived in England we discovered that you are blessed with this wonderful gulf stream that comes around the British Isles, and so it wasn't the big iceberg that I expected.

An Unusual Conference

But it was a strange conference. I went the whole week without actually ministering from the platform, although I met a few people during the week. The reason was that Michael decided that it was going to be one of those meetings where people just waited, and moved, and spoke, as the Spirit moved them. Anyone who felt led of the Lord could stand up and speak. Well, I thought to myself, the people here will expect me as an American woman to be the first one up, you know (because Americans have a reputation of being a little pushy) and so I said to my daughter, 'I'm going to fool them! I'm going to wait until a couple of the men have spoken, and then I'll speak.' But the thing was, nobody moved! It just went day after day with long periods of silence, now and then punctuated with a chorus or a hymn, or with someone reading Scripture.

It was the very early days of what is now commonly called the charismatic renewal. And there was a whole contingent of Church of Scotland ministers there on the back row who had been sent as observers of the renewal, and that's all they were doing: observing. They were watching very closely. Some Anglican bishops and canons were there as well. And everyone was just a little uneasy with everyone else, just a little cautious. So I finally thought to myself, 'I don't care if I do ruin my reputation — I really don't have any reputation to ruin. I'm just going to go ahead.' I had a lot to tell. God had done exciting things over on the Continent, and I wanted to share the good news. So two or three times I started to rise up and give a brief testimony about something that had happened, and a little voice came out of the crowd in the middle, and said, 'Be still.' My daughter collapsed with laughter. She said, 'Mum, to be interpreted, that means, "Shut up and sit down!" ' So I did, for the whole week.

At the end of the week, Michael turned and he said, 'This has been a strange conference.' And I thought, 'Well, you could say that again.' And then from the platform he said, 'We have some speakers whom you haven't met; for instance, there's a lady here from southern California, and she's a — ' and he kind of hesitated and said, 'What are you, Jean?' I was just a little diffident, and I stood up and said, 'Well, I'm just a handmaiden for the Lord, and everywhere I go if there are people reaching out for Jesus, I like to get their hands and the Lord's hands together.' And I sat down.

About two minutes later, the conference was over. And seven vicars came to me and asked me to come and minister in their churches. I knew that had to be the Lord: you know, ministers are very suspicious of itinerants coming through. No questions asked, but just a gracious invitation: 'Would you please come and minister in my church?' So I got on my knees in my room and laid my diary open before the Lord, and said, 'Lord, it's all in your hands.' I remembered La Donna's words, and I said, 'It looks like I'm going to stay here a while.' I proceeded then through those seven churches for several weeks, and God graciously blessed. They included St Cuthbert's in York where David Watson was just beginning his wonderful ministry in the power of the Spirit, and Birmingham Cathedral with David McGuinness. They were days in which tremendous ministries were being formed and released, and gifts of the Holy Spirit were being given to the church.

The Vision

During those weeks a vision came to me. It appeared three different times, during prayer, and it was the same vision each time. Now most of my revelation from the Lord is what I just 'know': He makes me know something, and I speak it forth. But now and then I have a vision, and when I do I have a pretty good one! Some people have a very garden variety type of visions: they're getting them all the time, you know. But I just have them now and then. And it's usually a milestone: a turning-point or very large directive in my life.

And what I saw was the British Isles, as in a bird's eye view. A kind of haze was over the whole, like a green fog. And then little pinpricks of light began to appear from the top of Scotland to Land's End. Then the Lord seemed to draw me closer to these lights, and I saw that they were fires that were burning. They were multiplying from the top of Scotland to Land's End. Then I saw lightning come and strike those fires, the brightest spots particularly, and there was a kind of explosion, and rivers of fire flowed down. Again, the sense of direction was from the top of Scotland to Land's End. But some of those rivers of fire didn't stop there. They went right across the Channel and spread out into the Continent.

The third time this vision appeared I figured the Lord was showing me or trying to tell me something. I was in Dorset by this time, at St Mary's (Church of England) with Rev Ken Prior, and I asked him if I could stay an extra day. You know, there's nothing quite so awkward as an evangelist the day after the meetings are over. But I said, 'Could I stay an extra day in the vicarage and pray? I need to find out what the Lord is trying to say to me.' Because up to that point I was really still on my way to Hongkong. And the Lord spoke to me very clearly. It was a wonderful day. It certainly changed the path of *my* life.

When I say the Lord spoke to me, I don't mean that it was an audible voice. But it was a knowing. That strong knowing, like reading the end of a book and knowing exactly what was going to happen. And you can't change it: it is written. And so it was written upon my heart, the meaning of this vision.

Phase One: The Glowing Fires

The Lord impressed it on my heart that those fires I saw were groups of people whom He would make intensely hungry for New Testament Christianity. They would start reading their Bibles and saying, for instance, as they read the book of Acts, 'Well, where is this happy church? Where are these people so full of the power of the Holy Spirit? Where are these miracles? Where is this growth, this vitality, this courage, this boldness, that these people had? Is that for today — can we have it today? Should the church be this way?'

And as these questions were being planted in their hearts, the Lord Jesus said He would make them very hungry for the Holy Spirit; He would fill them with the Holy Spirit and give them gifts of the Spirit, and out of those gifts would flow ministries that would enrich the Body of Christ. The whole concept of the Body of Christ would come alive, and barriers between denominations and different types of Christians would break down as people met each other.

The Lord said He would move these people all over the country. After He had taught them and given them gifts, He would move them to another place where they would carry that fire, and where they would meet others also who were being renewed by the Holy Spirit. He would put them in different situations from what they were used to, so that they would get to know people of other denominations, other cultures and other classes, and be able to communicate to them the blessings that the Lord had given them.

And then He told me that during that time He would also test them. There would be great testings of faith, great waiting times. He would teach them spiritual warfare. He would show them the meaning of the power of the blood of Jesus, the name of Jesus, the word of God and the power of the Holy Spirit.

Phase Two: The Coming of the Lightning

Then I asked the Lord, 'What does the lightning stand for?'

And He said, 'Unlike the first part, in which I will be speaking to Christians and preparing My church and renewing it and reviving the saints, the lightning represents a second part of the vision, in which I will bring a spiritual awakening to the nation that will be a witness to the unsaved, to the unchurched, to the non-Christian. Through these believers I will bring a witness to this land. They will be an army of witnesses. And I will begin to release their ministries so that when they give their testimonies there will be apostolic signs following and accompanying their testimonies. Where ears have been deaf and hearts have been hard and eyes have been blind, I will touch the people of this land and they will begin to hear the testimony of My people, they will begin to see the manifestations of My power, and their hearts will begin to believe. Thousands and thousands of people are going to come into My kingdom through this army of witnesses, through this people movement — not characterized by any particular evangelist or great organization at the front, but just My people rising up, led by My Spirit and beginning to move forward with a new faith for evangelism, a new zeal to share Jesus with others. And as they give their testimonies, I will release their ministries of healing and miracles, and there will be signs and wonders accompanying their ministries. So many people will be saved, in the villages as well as in the cities, in the schools, in the government, in media, in industry. It will affect the destiny of this nation, it will determine the course of the times.

Phase Three: Streams across the Channel

Then I said, 'Lord, what about these streams that go on across the Channel into Europe?'

And He said, 'That represents people who will rise up in the midst of this people movement, this army of witnesses in Britain, whom I will make My communicators.'

Now I hadn't used that word very much before in ministry. I said, 'Lord, what do you mean by communicators?'

And He said, 'They will not only be people endowed with the gifts of the Holy Spirit, with strong faith, but they will also be people talented in the arts. They will be writers, musicians, singers and actors, and also technicians in television, radio and the mass media. I will call and send them and put them in strategic places. I will bless their natural talents with My Spirit, and they will be *good*: they will excel. They will be leaders in their fields. I will send them into Europe, where they will meet other people in the media, and through them I will release the word of God very fast in Europe. The result will be another wave of a spiritual awakening, with thousands coming to Christ throughout Europe.'[2]

Well, I got kind of excited after I'd heard all that from the Lord, and I said, 'Lord, why are you telling me this? I'm on my way to Hongkong.' And He said, 'Oh, no, you're not: you're going to stay right here, and I'm going to bring Elmer here.'

And I said, 'What do you want us to do, Lord?'

And He said, '*I want you to nourish the fires that I light.*'

So I'm not the fire-lighter. The Lord is the fire-lighter.

A Time of Waiting

My husband was in Hongkong another year before he got here. But when he came, several pastors asked him if he would start a school for leadership training for people who had been filled with the Spirit and had gift ministries. He said, 'Well, I'll set it up for a year, and then we'll go back to the United States.' We forgot that we didn't have anything to go back to — you know, we'd sold the house and given away everything. I had given the money to the poorest people I could find — young preachers just starting out in the ministry. So there was nothing to go back to. But we still had that mind-set. It took a little while for the Lord to make us realize that He had other plans.

That was twenty-one years ago. And during those twenty-one years I have ministered all over this country, as Pastor Black has mentioned. But I have never gone away up to the north of Scotland. Many times I've said to my husband, 'I'd just love to go up there and find the fires that God has been lighting.' And he has said, 'Well, why don't you go on? I don't mind, if you want to go up there.' But I have said, 'No, I don't want to get ahead of the vision.' You know, it's very easy, when you get a revelation from God, to think you've got to go out and make it happen. That's very unwise — it doesn't bother God much, but it sure can be embarrassing for you. You can fall flat on your face. I've tried that a couple of times, and I think I've learned my lesson on it. So I said, 'No, I don't want to do anything like that. I want to go when the Lord really calls me to go, if He needs me.'

A Brush with Death

Last August our college sponsored a conference with a wonderful man of God named Judson Cornwall. Just before he came, I collapsed in a church service with a near-fatal coronary. Graham Kendrick was standing beside me; I was so glad he was there because he prayed for me right away, and I was wonderfully touched: instantly the pain subsided. It took me a little while, though, before I got home. I thought I had a bad case of indigestion! But the Lord did heal me, and I was able to attend the conference.

And a Revelation from Heaven

And one day, between lunch and the afternoon session, I said to our team, 'Let's just pray before we go upstairs.' I was thinking about very matter-of-fact things like how long should the worship go on, and where would we take the offering, and so on. I certainly wasn't thinking about visions and lights and fires. And suddenly the Spirit of God came upon me. I don't know if you've ever had anything like that where God's power and presence comes on you so mightily that suddenly everything else is forgotten. It wasn't that I couldn't have stopped: but I didn't want to. I began to weep and weep, and strong crying came upon my heart, real, deep sobs. I knew that the Spirit of God had brought the Lord's burden upon me. And I said, 'Lord, what is happening to me?' The closest thing I could compare to the intensity of the anointing that was upon me at that moment was when the Lord called me into the ministry when I was only fifteen years old. And I said, 'Lord, what is this? It's something very important.'

One word He spoke to me: *Scotland.*

Phase Two at Hand

Scotland. I knew what it meant. I knew that He wanted me to come up here, and I knew that He wanted me to come up with a special message. That message is to say to as many people as I can, in as many places as I can, that the second part of that vision is right at hand. It's here, folks, that spiritual awakening: it's starting, the very first signs of it are already upon us. Your generation are going to see a harvest of souls in this land such as you have never seen before. And it is going to have a tremendous effect not only upon this nation and the British Isles, but upon many other nations.

The First Sign: Men at Prayer[3]

There are three things that the Lord has asked me to share about this vision everywhere I go: three signs of this awakening. The first is that the Lord is sending a strong call to prayer among men. Early morning prayer meetings will start all over the land as men desire to pray, and they will start asking their pastors and leaders, 'Can we meet together before work to pray?' In those prayer meetings there will come strong intercession and an increased faith and vision in these men's souls for the nation. They will not only pray in their own churches, but soon they will start combining together in other churches, with other church groups. And in some places these prayer meetings will grow too big for the building, and they will come out in the open and pray in the parks or in front of town halls. Wouldn't that be nice, to have a prayer meeting right out here, of hundreds and hundreds of men lifting their voices in prayer for the nation? And it will be a sign in itself: these prayer meetings will be a witness to the nation, and many people will come to the Lord just by witnessing these prayer meetings, and hearing the prayers of these men.

The Second Sign: Christ Revealed to the Young

The second thing is that the Lord is going to send a tremendous revelation of Himself to boys and girls in this country. Between the ages of nine and fifteen particularly, children will begin to have a revelation of Jesus. They will see Him, they will know Him, they will hear Him, He will speak to them. He will come to them in visions and dreams, He will reveal His word to them. They will be converted and filled with the Holy Spirit and gifted by Him. And they will start praying. They will be healed themselves, and they will start praying for each other; and there will be wonderful healings through these boys and girls.

They will not only be the children of Christian parents. The Lord is going to manifest Himself to those who are in non-Christian homes where there is no love nor real family unity, where there is no knowledge of the Lord at all: perhaps not only for one generation but for many generations no Christian person has been in that family. But Jesus is going to meet them and reveal His power and His presence to them and His love for them. When they start coming to our children and to our teachers and telling what they are seeing and hearing from the Lord, our duty will be to receive them and love them as they are — because they will be rough diamonds, and they will have rather unusual, unchurchy language. But their experiences will be real. Some of their experiences will be so unusual you may doubt them. At that point receive their testimonies at face value, give them the word of God, and teach them how to love: because these children will have ministries not only as children, but as leaders in their adult life, and they will bless your country and other countries.

So receive these children, teach them. Those of you who teach Sunday school, those of you who have children in your home and neighbourhood whom you are concerned about, begin to ask the Lord to raise your level of expectation of what they can receive, because they are going to start hearing. And just like the adults, they will start hearing the word and receiving the Lord and being able to receive deep spiritual experiences in the Lord.

The Third Sign: Anointed Preachers

The third thing the Lord said He would do relates to the raising up of preachers. Although this awakening will not be characterized by great evangelists at the beginning, it will produce great preachers. You are going to hear anointed preaching, with a new sound in the church. You are going to hear evangelists with such fire, such powers of persuasion that they will touch thousands of people and win them to the Lord Jesus. God is giving these preachers not only to Scotland; He will send them to other parts of Britain, and many to other parts of the world, with an ever-increasing ministry of winning many people to the Lord.

Beware of Jealousy and Criticism

When the Lord reveals something to you, then you pray into it, not to make it happen, but to pray that as many people as possible will be involved and touched, and hear. And when I pray for this particular part of the vision, for these preachers and evangelists, I just feel the sorrow of Jesus' heart, for He says to me that He has already given to this land in recent times good ministries, strong ministries, that He wished to increase, but they were cut off, and hindered, and narrowed in the dimensions of their greatness because of jealousy, criticism and envy. In my spiritual warfare I have been coming against that spirit of jealousy, envy and criticism — because I think that it will try to rise up again, even in the face of the tremendous anointing God will give these preachers. So I just ask you to be on guard, be alert to that, and if you feel those feelings and emotions rising up in you against some ministry that God is blessing, be generous in your heart, be quick to repent of it, and ask the Lord to take that away, so that you can contribute and nourish and support those ministries, rather than stand back from them with hostility and jealousy. The Lord is going to use them, whether you like them or not. But it would be a lot better if you liked them and got right in there beside them, because then you could share the joy of winning souls for the Lord Jesus — because that's what it's all about, folks.

The Lord isn't sending us for fun and games, any more than He sent the charismatic renewal for us to have holy huddles and exchange spiritual gifts like Christmas presents all the time. That isn't the purpose of the renewal. The purpose is evangelism. It's to get out there into that harvest that God is preparing. And you sons and daughters of Scotland, the Lord wants to raise you up and make you part of this great move of the Spirit in modern times. What is going to happen in Scotland will be part of a modern missionary movement that will bless the whole world, and Scotland will greatly contribute to this. So be part of it.

A Deluge of Power

You young people, you are going to see miracles and effective ministry such as our eyes have never seen, as the Lord pours out His Spirit, not only upon the Christians, but upon the unsaved, in these days. So be encouraged. Jesus said men ought always to pray and never give up — because this harvest is bound to include some of your friends, some of your neighbours, your families, who need the Lord. So have faith, have courage.

Take Courage

When I first came to England, Jeanne Harper met me, and drove us from Heathrow in a little Mini car, riding on the wrong side of the road, you know! My daughter and I had five pieces of luggage each — we thought we needed all of that — and so the car was heaped up inside and out with all this luggage. As Jeanne was driving furiously through the peak-hour traffic, my heart was thumping, first because I was excited to be here, and secondly because of all the traffic and double-decker buses and everything.

I looked out over the tops of the cases and saw a great big red sign with gold letters, saying, *Courage! Take courage!* And I said to her, 'Isn't it wonderful how your government has put up all these morale boosters!' She said, 'Oh, these are ale advertisements.' I said, 'Oh, well, I'll take it in the right spirit!'

So have courage, folks: take courage, and know that God is with us, and He has chosen to cause our eyes to see things that He has prepared for us in this age that are beyond anything we could ask or think. He will do it, according to the power that works mightily in us as His church. Praise the Lord.

Mr Black's Comments on the Occasion

It is one thing to have a clear-cut vision. But there is a difference between having a clear-cut vision and actually voicing it in such detail and with such authority as Jean has done. It takes faith, it takes courage, and indeed I think we must all be very deeply impressed with what we have heard. As it happened, I had heard about this vision probably very soon after she had first spoken of it. I knew of it, not in detail but in general; I believed it then, and I believe it now. I do believe that there will come a tremendous awakening in this land before the Lord comes, and I thank you tonight, Jean, for putting things so strongly, so clearly. I would ask the congregation to listen carefully and to take courage from what you have heard.

Jean Darnall Resumes

It's lovely to have that little break, because in many places I have been on my feet for about an hour-and-a-half, between telling the vision and giving the appropriate word for each place. For I have asked the Lord to keep the testimony fresh. When you are telling the same testimony over and over again, you pray, 'Lord, don't let it become just like a tape-recording.' I don't feel that way in my heart: I get thrilled and blessed and excited every time I tell it, but I don't want my voice to sound as though I have told it before. And I hope that it felt fresh to you tonight.

How many of you felt a witness in your heart, that it said something that you had heard before? It wasn't brand new, the Lord had given you some clues along the same line. I just wish I had time to hear all of the visions and the words and the revelations the Lord has given you — it would make a beautiful mural, wouldn't it? It would be like little tiles fitting together to form a big mosaic — because everywhere I go I've had people come up to me and speak of their experiences in connection with revival.

I was in the little fishing village of Mallaig, across from Skye, having lunch in a lady's home, when she said, 'I want to bring together the people that have been praying for revival in our home.' There were a couple of fishermen's wives there, and when I mentioned the men's prayer meetings, one of the women got so excited and said, 'That's started on the ships, on the fishing boats! They're starting prayer meetings. It has spread to several of the boats there.' Now that's really revival already on its way, isn't it? Little things like that all along have added to the picture of what God is saying. This call to prayer among men is certainly happening already in different places. One place had these men's prayer meetings going on for two years, and the pastor said, 'I thought it would be something that would just dwindle out after a few weeks, but it's stronger than ever!' So where you see these signs, then flow with it, folks. Don't fight it, go with it and be part of it, and let the Lord bless you.

Notes

[1] An earlier account of Jean Darnall's vision of revival is given in her book, *Heaven, Here I Come* (Lakeland, 1974), pp. 112–14).

[2] As with various of the predictions in Jean's vision, this one is not what we might naturally have expected to be a feature of a coming revival. It forms no part of a recurring pattern.

In Colin Whittaker's *Great Revivals*, there is an interesting passage with a remarkably similar emphasis:

...there is a growing conviction among men and women of the Spirit that we are at last moving into God's time for an outpouring of the Spirit upon Britain and America. When God speaks, He never leaves us with just one witness, it is a divine principle that every word shall be established by two or three witnesses (2 Corinthians 13:1). Furthermore, God always chooses reliable and proven witnesses when He wishes to reveal something to His people. It is therefore very thrilling to find so many voices saying the same thing — namely that God's time for revival is at hand.

Witness number one is the Rev. Henry Brash Bonsall, M.A., B.D., the highly respected Principal of the Birmingham Bible Institute. In the Winter [1983] issue of the College Magazine *Gateway*, he wrote, 'We as a College are poised in preparation for the Revival which God showed me fifty years ago He was going to send to this country. In this Revival, He has revealed, it is not so much religious people that will be converted but leaders in industry, professional life, political life, and experts. These will be people who have never darkened a church door and have not the scintilla of an idea of what Christ really is. To such He will be revealed. Revival means God coming to a community face-to-face when the hearts of hardest rock will

flow down like lava, and men will be called to be God's servants to the ends of the earth. They will come to this, and every available college, demanding instant training.'
See Colin Whittaker, *Great Revivals*, pp. 177–8.

3 The three signs are given in the order in which Jean Darnall related them. Whether they would occur in the same temporal order was not actually stated, although their internal content might seem to suggest this.

8 | IN THE SERVICE OF THE KING

[What follows is the sermon Jean Darnall preached on the occasion of her visit to the City Halls, Glasgow in June 1987, after she had concluded her comments on the vision.]

I thought that I would like to share with you tonight from some scriptures that the Lord has been giving me along the road. When I first started on this five week tour, my regular Bible reading was in First Chronicles. I stayed there a little longer than usual, because every day it seemed that the Lord was putting more into my heart about what to pray and ask for. I have found that it has become a message not only to me; I feel that it can be a message to you tonight. It's not very well outlined and homiletical, but I think it will be inspirational! My daughter once was asked if, when she grew up, she was going to be a preacher like her mother, and she said, 'No, like my daddy!' On being asked, 'Well, don't you think of your mother as a preacher?' she said, 'No, my mother's no preacher. She's an inspirator.' Of course she knew that my husband always had everything really well outlined, and I would sometimes just stand up and talk!

The Service of the King

Now I want you to look at First Chronicles, chapter twelve. I'd like to think of this as related to 'the service of the King'. When I became a Christian at the age of fifteen, after being miraculously healed, I read a book entitled *In the Service of the King*. I liked that little phrase so much that it became my signature phrase. I would sign my letters, 'In the service of the King, Jean Darnall'. Then my daughter when she was in her teens (there's nothing smarter than a thirteen-year-old, have you noticed that? They really know everything) said, 'Mom, that's kind of old-fashioned: "In the service of the King". You ought to shorten that just a little bit.' So now I just write, 'In His service'. But it means the same thing. He's still King, isn't he? And He's the King of kings, but He's also the King of our lives personally. He's going to be King of kings in a total, universal way, but right now as we open our hearts to Him He is the King of my life; I hope He's the King of your life.

Chosen and Anointed

Here in First Chronicles we have the story of a transition period for David. He had been anointed as a boy when Samuel came to his father's home, sent by God to anoint someone king. All the older sons had been paraded, and Samuel said, 'No, no, not that one, not that one,' and finally he said, 'Jesse, don't you have any more sons?' He said, 'Well, the youngest one is out there in the fields with the sheep.' Samuel said, 'Well, bring him in.' And they brought in the shepherd boy, named David. As soon as Samuel saw him, the Lord said, 'That's the one.' The Lord knows whom He wants, doesn't He? He knows whom He wants, and He'll go through a lot of different steps in order to get His hand upon that one whom He wants to use. He wants us all, but He chooses us for different things. Jesus said, 'You have not chosen Me: I have chosen you, and I have ordained you that you should bring forth fruit.' It is a wonderful thing when not only does God know whom he wants to use and how He wants to use them, but also the one whom He chooses knows that he is chosen. When you get that sense of chosenness, that touch of the hand of the Lord on your life, it is the most precious thing that could ever happen to you.

I left Bible college about six months before graduating, because my husband had already graduated: it was the war years, and he had to pick a church or else he was going to be drafted into the army. He decided he wanted to be in the Lord's army rather than the US army, so I left college with him and we went to pastor. Then we went to Panama and Australia. We started churches and Bible schools, and about eleven years after I had left college we were called back to Angelus Temple in Los Angeles, where I was asked to take a position as a pastor. But when they got out my files, they found out that I had never graduated, which meant I had never been ordained. They said, 'Oh, my goodness, we can't put you on as pastor of Angelus Temple unless you are duly ordained!' Of course, I carried my husband's ordination because we ministered together. So I said to them, 'Oh, it doesn't matter; I know the Lord has ordained me.' They said, 'Yes, but we need to recognize that you are ordained.' And I didn't ever know how important that was, until the day that I was ordained by the church.

It was a wonderful experience. I remember Dr Macpherson came along with the elders, and they were anointing all of these new preachers who had been out for one year after they graduated (they have to minister for a year, and then come back, before they are ordained). I was standing there, a sort of senior candidate, having already done considerable service. I had been preaching before I ever went to Bible college; I had preached since I was sixteen years of age. But there I stood, and there came the leaders of the church, and they laid hands on me. And I fell under the power of God, along with about fifty or sixty others. The floor was carpeted with those who were ordained that day. Every one fell under the power of God.

It was a couple of hours before I got up on my feet. The Lord showed me many things about my future during those hours. But the strangest thing happened the next evening. My husband and I went to another church to minister. As our custom was, we knelt to pray before standing to minister. As I was about to stand, I felt a hand come upon my head. I had had hands laid upon me the day before, and had been anointed with oil. So now I thought, 'I wonder why Elmer is reaching over and putting his hand on my head.' But when I looked over, he had both of his hands up to his face, praying. I realized that the Lord was making me conscious that His hand was upon me. And, you know, that stayed with me for weeks. Every time I went to minister, that hand was upon me. Although I don't feel it physically tonight, I know it is there. Friends, if you have had God touch your life, walk worthy of the calling wherewith you have been called.

David had that experience: he had those hands laid on him and the anointing oil come upon him. As a boy he knew that he was chosen.

And Then the Conflict

You would have thought that David would have gone straight from that farm to the throne, wouldn't you? But not by a long shot. Have you ever noticed that everybody that God chose and called and ordained to do something special for Him in the Scriptures had to fight for the job He gave him to do? Right away there would be conflict. You may think that if God calls you, everything's going to go fine. But you can be sure that there will be immediate counteraction, both human and otherwise, against your calling. God allows that: it isn't accidental, or incidental. God allows it, to prove to you your commitment to the calling and the choice that He has made. You make sure that you choose to be chosen. David went through those years of exile, being hated and pursued by King Saul.

Even though he had been a national hero and had slain Goliath, he still had to run for his life from the jealousy and the envy of this king who was out of God's will.

The Outcasts Gather to David

But during that time, he had men come around him wherever he would hide away, in caves and different places. Men would come to him, and they were often men on the run, men who themselves were fugitives from either injustice or justice, trouble and debt and so forth. And they identified with David. They were a motley group; they weren't really trained soldiers or extra-special people, but they just were drawn to him. They stayed with him and camped with him at different places. So all along the line were being developed these friends of the future king. They learned to know him and to know his heart. They felt his heart, and came under his anointing by identifying themselves with him. They would begin to share his vision for Israel; his dreams became their dreams.

And then one day a runner came to David and told him that Saul and Jonathan had died in battle. Now David could go ahead and be what God wanted him to be.

Touch Not the Lord's Anointed

David said, 'How do you know for sure that Saul is dead?' The runner said, 'I with my own hand, upon Saul's request, finished him off because he had tried to commit suicide and bungled the job. He asked me to slay him, and I did.' And David said, 'Weren't you afraid to touch God's anointed?' Now Saul was out of God's will; he was not acting as he should; he was sinning against the anointing that had been put upon him. Nevertheless he was the one that God had allowed to be king for that season. And David said, 'Weren't you afraid to touch him?' There had been a couple of other occasions in David's life when he could have slain Saul, and refrained. The men who were around him saw it: they saw that terribleness in him, that loyalty to the anointing that he recognized and would not touch.

Gathering Forces

Now he was released, and he started to think about what he was going to do. There is a very interesting passage in 1 Chronicles 12 that speaks of 'the mighty men, helpers in war'.

Now these were the men who came to David at Ziklag while he was still a fugitive from Saul the son of Kish; and they were among the mighty men, helpers in the war, armed with bows, using both the right hand and the left in hurling stones and shooting arrows with the bow. They were of Benjamin, Saul's brethren.... Some Gadites joined David at the stronghold in the wilderness, mighty men of valor, men trained for battle, who could handle shield and spear, whose faces were like the faces of lions, and were as swift as gazelles on the mountains.... Then some...came to David at the stronghold. And David went out to meet them, and answered and said to them, 'If you have come peaceably to me to help me, my heart will be united with you; but if to betray me to my enemies, since there is no wrong in my hands, may the God of our fathers look and bring judgment.' Then the Spirit came upon Amasai, chief of the captains, and he said, 'We are yours, O David; we are on your side, O son of Jesse! Peace, peace to you, and peace to your helpers! For your God helps you.' So David received them, and made them captains of the troop.... And they helped David against the bands of raiders, for they were all mighty men of valor, and they were captains in the army. For at that time they came to David day by day to help him, until it was a great army, like the army of God (1 Chron 12:1–22: NKJV).

There were those *who had the understanding of the times, to know what Israel ought to do* (v.32).

They were stout-hearted men, who could keep ranks:

All these men of war, who could keep ranks, came to Hebron with a loyal heart, to make David king over all Israel; and all the rest of Israel were of one mind to make David king (v.38).

The last words of that chapter are: *For there was joy in Israel.* There is nothing more joyful than when men and women in God's family are of one heart and one mind to make Jesus King, to make Him Lord, to honour Him, and to recognize what He is doing, and to say, as these men said to David, 'We are Yours, O Lord. We are on Your side, Son of God. Peace, peace to You, and peace to Your helpers, for we know that Your God, Your Father, helped You.'

We have seen how Jesus came as the commander-in-chief, you might say, as the captain of our salvation. He proved Himself in the greatest battle of all, against Satan at the cross, and won that marvellous victory, and He is worthy of our loyalty, worthy of our courageous service around Him. He calls us. And I believe that at this time, just as we need to be loyal to the Lord Jesus, so we need to be loyal to one another as people of God, and to recognize that all of us, as those who have come into the kingdom of God, have been anointed and touched by the Holy Spirit. We should have a respect for the Holy Spirit and His anointing in each other's lives. And we should be particularly fearful of touching those whom God has anointed for leadership.

I sense that this is an important message, and I have chosen to bring this word tonight to this, one of the largest gatherings I have spoken to in Scotland, because I sense something about great ministries — this is a time for greatness. Greatness in God's heart will allow people to be anointed and used by Him in a wonderful way. But it's a time for us to have a great sense of loyalty, a great sense of love and oneness and unity, to be big-hearted, to have big minds so that we don't narrow ourselves down to trivia. As someone has said, David was a giant-killer, not a midge-killer! Many of us go through life swatting at midges, when we should be killing giants. We are fighting little, squabbly things that annoy us and irritate us, when we need to be using our fervour, our words, and our feelings against the enemy, and pulling down the strongholds of Satan. What God wants and what David needed around him, was an army. Although he was anointed, although he was called by God, he could never have been the king who united the kingdom and who united the nation, without this loyal army. He needed these men.

Becoming a Great Army

Now what interests me is this. How did this band of mercenaries become the great army that God is describing here? These mighty men of valour, these men who are strong and skilful in war, these men who could throw sling-shots with the left hand and the right hand? The rocks weren't paltry little toys; they were a phenomenon of nature. In the British Museum you will see samples: larger than cricket balls, they are perfectly round stones that have been shaped by avalanches or glaciers or running water. There is a little tag under several specimens which says, 'Stones such as David probably used when he slew the giant Goliath'. No wonder he fell over: it must have made a hole right through his head, you know! But the skill and the strength to throw that accurately and hit the enemy just on target was amazing. And these men imitated David. They admired him, and so they decided they wanted to be good 'sling-shotters'. They learned how to throw those stones not only with the right hand, but also with the left. They learned how to attack the enemy from whichever side he came. Now when did they learn all that? How did they become so expert? In that waiting period: in that exile time. In that time when they were a hidden people, when they were not official, when they were just friends of this man named David.

Preparing Ourselves for Battle

You are Jesus people: you are friends of Jesus. Many of you have been waiting and going through hard times where you have had to practise your 'sling-shotting'. They made their own weapons, they made spears, they made shields, they learned how to fight defensively with shields and they learned how to fight offensively with their spears. They were practising all that time. When the king needed them, they were ready.

That is why you have been tested. That is why you have had to wait. That is why the Lord has allowed you to be in that place where your ministry seemed to be held back, where your zeal was in a narrow place and unable fully to express itself, where you were forced to your knees to hold on to the promises of God, where you have become skilful in binding and loosening the enemy and pulling down strongholds, where you were forced to look up all the scriptures on spiritual warfare and read of the victory in Jesus and the power of His name and His blood, and to understand the effectiveness of the word of God, where you went to Ephesians and found your armour, and put on the helmet of salvation and the shield of faith and the breastplate of righteousness, and bound about yourself that girdle of truth, and shod your feet with the preparation of the gospel of peace. You have had your shoes on ready to run for a long time, but you couldn't run. There was no room for you: you were in a narrow place. But God is ready to bring you into a large place.

It says here that these men had faces like lions. That means they were brave, they were strong, they held themselves regally. The lion, you know, is considered to be the king of the forest. They had the bearing of those who belonged to the king, and they had the courage of those who knew that their king was anointed and destined for greatness. And they would share his greatness.

Saints of God, you are destined to share the greatness of your Lord. When He manifests His power in this country, He wants you to be His loyal soldiers. He wants you to be in His army. He's going to use those talents, those abilities, those spiritual skills that He has been developing in you, the scriptures that you have learned, the promises He has put in your heart. They are all part of your armour and your weapons for this spiritual warfare and great victory. There will be many captives to bring out of captivity; there will be many souls needing to be set free by powerful prayers and anointed ministry. And this testing time, this waiting time, has been in preparation for making you God's army. Lay hold on the occasion. Bring all of your talents to the Lord to be sanctified and to be put into the Master's service. Learn patience. Learn constancy. Learn much discipline; receive it from the Lord, and say, 'Father, I know that You are doing this to me. You are cutting me back, You are pruning me for more fruitfulness. You are allowing this test in my life because You love me.' And instead of cringing and complaining, say, 'Lord, I just want to thank You that I am Your son, and I am Your daughter, because in the last days You will pour out Your Spirit on all flesh, and on Your sons and upon Your daughters, and they shall prophesy.' Upon His maidservants and upon His menservants in those days shall He pour out His Spirit.

Fight discouragement. Remember this: that just before the greatest victories that God gives in our lives, the devil (who doesn't know everything, but has a strong sense of what is about to happen), will come and load you down and hit you hard with an overdose of discouragement and despair. He will bring people around you who will be the best pessimists in the land, and they will just pour it upon you. He will try to create disloyalty amongst those that you need so desperately in your dark hour. When you feel that loneliness, and when you feel that terrible discouragement upon you, that is the time to lift up your head and overcome in the name of Jesus. Be true to the calling that God has given you. Know that the Lord has received you. As David said here, 'If you come to me to help me, my heart will be united with you.' And that is what salvation is: a fusion of the life of Jesus and your life together. *He who is the Lord's is one spirit with him.* United with Him, fused with Him. And that is what the Lord is calling for now. Some of you are playing games, you know. You are playing church. And it won't do, because the Lord wants your loyalty, the Lord wants your commitment. He wants you to say, 'Yes, Lord, I recognize that You are my anointed King, the Saviour of my soul.'

Human Need

I was talking to a young man earlier today who has been looking into all kinds of religions and trying everything. He is wasting his life: he is a wanderer. And his body is wasting away; he has been on drugs and only the Lord knows what else. This young man has talent, and you can tell that he has had a good brain, but it's so confused with so much deception, and also with lies from the enemy about who he is and what he can do and what he can't do. I said to him, 'Richard, wait a minute. I don't need to hear all of that. I have heard that, I have studied that for years. I could tell you more about that than you have ever learned. But what I want to know is, what do you think of Jesus Christ?' And of course that was the crunch, because he disliked the very name of Jesus, and when he said hateful things about Jesus' name, I said, 'Don't say that: that hurts me. He is my dearest friend; I love Him. If you get yourself lined up with Jesus, then all these other problems will come clear to you. To settle this confusion, He is the key.'

Divine Provision

The cross is the key as well. Jesus and His cross: that's the key. As long as He's Jesus the teacher He's just fine. But that isn't what I am talking about just now. I am talking about Jesus the Saviour, Jesus the One who says, *If any man will be my disciple, let him deny himself, and take up his cross, and follow me.* That sounds hard, doesn't it? Sounds as though it'll just be all loss...Oh, no, it won't. If you deny yourself and take up your cross and follow Jesus, you come into His army, into His kingdom, into His glory, and He shares His victory and His blessings with you. Just now the call is for faithful service. Those of you who are in the service of the Lord and are discouraged, I want to encourage not to give up. Stay true to where you are. Develop your skills for the Lord, in prayer and loving people and forgiving people and reconciling people. Develop the face of a lion, of those who will not back down, those who know that they belong to the King.

Swift as Gazelles

These people *were as swift as gazelles on the mountains.*

Just yesterday morning I was sitting in a garden by a loch, where I had gone early to pray. I looked up, and there came a stag walking out across the clearing in the field next to me. He stopped and looked around and oh, he was so beautiful. He did a kind of reconnaissance out there. Then he came back into the little glen that was next to me. And I sat perfectly still; I didn't want to disturb such a glorious creature, he was so beautiful. Then all of a sudden out came the doe, and she stood there, ever so still and just trembling in that early morning light. Then she went back. And then they both came out with little baby Bambi — he was so tiny — and he came out, looking around. It was a lovely family. But you know, I moved a little bit, because I thought, 'Oh, I've just got to see them a little better' — and with the slightest movement, away they were. They were gone like a flash of lightning.

And I said, 'Oh, Lord, give us feet like that. Make us ready, not to run away in fear, but so that when the time comes for this awakening we will be swift to move, we won't be hindered, we won't be clumsy, but we will be ready to go for God.'

Responding to the Call

Some of you are so tied up with the cares of this world, so squinty-eyed with cynicism and unbelief that you have lost that ability to react to the call of the Lord. I call upon you: ask the Lord to give you open-eyed faith, that you will look at Jesus with the eyes of a child, full of wonder, full of love, and worship Him and adore Him. Be loyal to Him, love Him, learn His heart, learn how He thinks, how He feels about this world, share His dream, share His plan to bless this nation, and be His loyal soldier. Be ready to take the place the King has for you, whether it be a humble place amongst the troops, or whether it be one of the captains in the forefront. Whatever the position, God knows where you will be your very best: and that is the important place to be.

Day by day, the Lord brought these soldiers out of the bushes, out of the mountains, out of the caves, out of the unknown places, and brought them to the king, and by joining with the king they became great, a great army, like God's army. And He is calling you to greatness: greatness of love, greatness of life, greatness of living and forgiving. I hope that you will answer that call, right now, in your hearts. Shall we bow our heads in prayer?

> PRAYER [JD]: *Lord, we want to take the challenge, and we want to take the responsibility that You are giving us today. Lord, we want to say as these men did to David, 'David, we are on your side. Jesus, we are on Your side. We are one with You, Lord. Yes, Lord, bless*

*this land and use me for Your glory the way You want
to. Lord, give me understanding of my times.' Give us,
Lord, knowledge of Your strategy for this city. O Jesus,
You have a plan for Glasgow. You have a plan for this
region here, a strategy that will need to draw together
Your troops, Your people. Lord, we thank You for
what You have been teaching them all through these
years about the Word, about the Holy Spirit, about
prayer, and about their need of one another, about the
gifts of the Spirit, about the body of Christ. Lord, You
have poured such wonderful teaching into our lives.
Now, Lord, help us to do something with it. Help us to
use it, Lord, to bless this nation as we serve You
together, stout-hearted and keeping our ranks. Lord
Jesus, those that kept their ranks kept in step, and
when they faced the enemy they didn't break up, they
stayed together, they held their shields together, they
used their swords together.*

*Lord Jesus, I pray tonight for those that the enemy
is tempting to break ranks, to run away from the
conflict, to run away from accountability, to run away
from responsibility, to give up their calling, to be
disloyal to You and to those who trust them. Lord, I
come against that spirit tonight that is working
throughout this area. I felt it as I drove into this region
today, Lord Jesus, and Your Spirit prayed through me
against that spirit that is creating disloyalty, breaking
up the ranks of God's people. Lord, You are bringing
them together, but the enemy is sending this division,
this suspicion, this criticism, this envy, this jealousy.
Lord, it's not only in the church; it's in our homes, it's
in families; and I come against it in the name of Jesus.
And, Lord, I pray that just now the blessed Holy Spirit
will sweep over us and release us and forgive us
through the blood of Jesus and cleanse us from all the
contamination of this attack of the enemy. And, Lord,
unite us, bring us together and give us a holy
reverence for the anointed of God, for those who serve
you in the power of the Spirit, Lord Jesus, those you
have chosen amongst us and raised up to lead forth
into the battle. Give us great hearts to receive all*

whom You will give us in the days ahead, Lord, from whatever direction they come, in Jesus' name.

Then I pray, Lord Jesus, for young people here particularly, whom the world is wooing and drawing, the world that is so full of despair, the world that is so full of deception. Lord Jesus, I pray for those young people who are depressed, and also disheartened, who are already fighting deep despair as if they were old before their time: they have that sense of helplessness, that sense of futility. Lord Jesus, I pray for them, that You will lift up their eyes to see You, glorious and victorious, with a plan for each of their lives, and with the power to live it out, dear Lord Jesus; and that they will not lack anything they will need, to be the men and the women You want them to be. You will provide, dear Lord. You give them the Holy Spirit, You give them cleansing and deliverance from all manner of sickness and defeat in their lives, a new mind, a new body, a new heart, Lord. And I thank You for it.

APPEAL [JD]

To All in Need: *While our heads are bowed, I am going to speak to those of you who say, 'Jean, I need that new heart, I need that new life that Jesus gives, I want my life to be meaningful and significant, and I don't have it in myself. I am in bondage to sin, I am in bondage to things that already defeat me and would destroy me. But I need victory and deliverance through the King, through the anointed One, through the Saviour, and somehow my heart is drawn to Him; the Holy Spirit has caused me to want to be with Him, and to walk with Him and to live for Him; and I would like to give my life for Him as He was willing to give His life for me.' I wonder how many there are who will say, 'Yes, I want to accept Jesus as my Saviour and my Lord, to live my life in the service of the King, and I offer myself to Him now. I want to bring every talent, not only the good things of my life, but the bad things as well: all of me, I want to offer to the Lord Jesus, for cleansing, refining and purifying, so that He can make*

*me the man or the woman that He wants me to be.
Yes, I am coming to Jesus. I want to be identified with
the Lord Jesus Christ. I want to serve Him, and I want
Him to make me a loyal person.*

To the Weak and Unfaithful: *I sense in someone here a
strain of unfaithfulness, because you have had a great
model of unfaithfulness in your family, and you don't
know whether you've got it in you to be faithful to God
or man. There is just that weakness in you, and you
are afraid of it. Oh, my friend, the Lord can change
your heart and give you a strong sense of loyalty and
steadfastness and faithfulness to God and to
whomever He gives you to love and to be with in this
life. He can make you a faithful husband, a faithful
wife. He'll make you faithful to your parents and
children, faithful to your family. He wants to take that
hostility out of you, that lack of respect out of you,
and give you a deep sense of respect and loyalty and
love for others.*

*I sensed that so strongly today when I came into
this city. I was praying in the car as I came across the
Erskine Bridge. The Spirit of God came upon me, and I
just saw homes and families and churches being
broken up by disloyalty, by an inability to stand up
under battle, breaking ranks, running away from each
other and the enemy. God wants to unite you, put a
courage in your hearts. Are there those who say, 'Yes, I
know I've broken rank in one way or another: I need
that. I'm a runaway.' But God has not given us the
spirit of fear, but of love and power and a sound mind
(2 Tim 1:7). And if you are confused and unable to
concentrate and get any goals in your life and you are
just drifting, the Lord wants to bring into your life an
understanding of who you are and of His plan for you,
so that you can have goals and move towards them
with courage. Don't be a drifter, don't be a fugitive.
Become a soldier for the King.*

To the Hurting: *Some of you have been misunderstood
and misjudged. You have come under that cruel lash*

of criticism and jealousy, and you're hurt; you're deeply hurt. The Lord wants to heal that so that you do not carry any bitterness in you, or give up or lose the place that the Lord has put you in. The Lord knows where He can use you best, and if He has put you there, oh, I just pray for you that your faith will not fail, that you will be steadfast, unmovable, ever abounding in the work of the Lord. I feel that there are hurt and wounded people here, and I don't know, but maybe the ones who wounded you are sitting near you. If that is so, may the Holy Ghost come upon all of you, and may this be a time of healing and reconciliation. I would like you to respond and say, 'Yes, I need healing. I need forgiveness and help right now.'

And if you have been the criticizer, if you have fallen prey to becoming a tool of the enemy (we've all done it, we've all been weak, and sometimes appointed ourselves as judges) and the Lord has touched your heart and convicted you of that, you just need to say, 'Lord, forgive me, and cleanse my heart of this, in the name of Jesus. I don't want this to be a master in my life.'

[A very large number of people came forward for prayer, stretching right across the main City Halls from wall to wall.]

CLOSING SPECULATION

As I have sought to show, there are quite definite and recurring patterns in revival and also age-abiding principles. Past experience, however, also reveals that from time to time quite unique features emerge, as for example in the Rwanda Revival (see *Revival: Personal Encounters*). And very obviously Jean Darnall envisages new things.

One revival which I have not included in my review but which has considerably influenced my thinking is described in Mel Tari's book *Like a Mighty Wind* (Coverdale House Publishers Ltd., 1973; first published by Creation House, 1971). Not only does it tell of unique features, but it seems to me to give pointers to what we may increasingly expect as we come nearer the end of the age: an increase in phenomenal miracles, to the extent that these will be undeniable. In the Indonesian revival there is no doubt that the dead were raised as in New Testament times, and water was turned to wine — again and again. The power of witchdoctors was totally subdued by the power operating in God's servants. The miraculous and the phenomenal were undeniable.

In my view, open and astonishing miracle will accompany revival in our own and other lands as we come nearer the end. For this I believe we should prepare and to this end we should pray. This generation perhaps more than any other needs to be shocked into an awareness of the reality of God.

I would again like to draw readers' attention to the remarkable visitation of God in Minnesota in which Mr Ian Andrews was very recently used. As this book goes to press I have only partial information of the present situation, but I have obtained a tape of an address given by Mr Andrews to a Full Gospel Fellowship which contains details of quite phenomenal happenings.

To my mind there are clear pointers to the glorious nature of what God is preparing for His people. We see the cloud already bending and anticipate the coming floods.

While I have drawn attention to past revivals and their common features, I do think we should now condition our thinking to things new. There can be a danger in trying to replicate the past. In this context the words used in another setting may be very relevant: *Things which eye saw not, and ear heard not, And which entered not into the heart of man, Whatsoever things God prepared for them that love him* (1 Cor 2:9).

And, finally, surely the words used in relation to the coming of Christ and its effect on us can be similarly used of our attitude to revival: *And every one that hath this hope set on him purifieth himself, even as he is pure* (1 Jn 3:3).

APPENDIX I

Purity Brings the Glory Down

[The following was given as a preliminary exhortation by Miss Mary Black before the first address in this book.]

There is such a straight and simple connection between the revealing of the glory of God and the purifying of the individual life. This place would be blazing with glory if every life were pure. Impurity is probably one of the greatest stumbling blocks between the soul and God. When you look at a glass of water and you are considering drinking it, if you detect just the slightest sign of impurity in that water, a fleck of dirt that has got into it, you empty the glass out and get another supply. Impurity in what we drink, we will just not tolerate. And neither will God. I wonder, as He comes to your life and mine to take a drink, if He has to pass on because the water is impure?

Sometimes as I look into the eyes, especially of young people today, I have to look away quickly. It is almost as if I am hit with uncleanness in the expression of the eyes: lust, sexual lust in particular. And it is in the church of Christ. If I cannot bear to look, I who am a creature of the fallen race, what is it for Christ, who comes to have communion with His own, and finds in the eyes of His people that look of longing for physical satisfaction in the lusts of the flesh, a craving that is carnal? What a wound it must be to Christ, and what an inward change for men when purity is embraced — what an incoming of the glory of God.

He can come and rest on our lives when we have
cleaned them up, when we have really cleaned them up.
It is fashionable nowadays for our young folks to speak of
a 'problem'. 'I've got this problem. I keep thinking these
thoughts; this is my problem.' We'd rather call it a problem than sin, wouldn't we? A problem sounds quite
respectable: anybody can have a problem. Just call it sin.
Immoral thoughts are just sin. They are not a problem;
they are sin, and you are responsible to get rid of them,
because the blood of Christ and the grace of God has
flowed for you. If you want to be clean you can be clean; if
you are not clean you have chosen not to be clean, and
you are missing so much of the incoming of the glory of
the Lord.

Sin is Death

If we thought we were in danger of catching a dread and
fatal physical disease by touching a certain substance, if
we knew that it was going to kill us within six hours of
touching it, how would we react? If I had a cupful of some
muddy-looking substance, and I said, 'You know, if you
touch that you will die within the hour,' would you not be
careful? I know of somebody who has an allergy to a
certain kind of food, and if they even touch that food, not
eat it but just touch it with their hand, they will die in
twenty minutes, unless they get immediate hospital attention and an injection of an antidote. They have twenty
minutes to live from the point of contact. Imagine yourself
to be that person, and I have the substance here. How
many of you would run forward to experiment, to put
your finger in it, to see if it works, to see if it kills you in
twenty minutes' time — if it's as bad as I say? I don't think
you would; I think you would run from it. And if you
heard that to be within a radius of ten yards would put
you in danger, you would be outwith that radius in ten
seconds. You wouldn't be seeing how near you could get

to it without falling over; you'd be seeing how far away you could get, and you probably wouldn't come back next week to the church because there was such a fool at the front holding up this dangerous substance that might have killed half the congregation! We would feel real about it, and we would be real about it, if our body was in danger.

And sin is death. Uncleanness and immorality and unclean thoughts are death to your soul, and you are experimenting, just to see. You have a wee nibble at it — you go as near as you can, instead of staying as far away as you can. And it shows in your eyes, the death that is already working in your spiritual life.

Purity is Life

I can tell as soon a person begins actually to practise inward purity. In a meeting such as this they are alive, vitally alive. Their eyes sparkle with light, joy, livingness. There is that vital quality of being alive — because purity brings the revelation of the glory of the Lord. Dead eyes tell of sin — you know these dead, lacklustre, 'wish-I-wasn't-here' eyes: they tell that the story of your inner life is sin. Purity brings the glory down. Reach out at least in your will and your choice for that purity, and follow it through with action.

> And the glory of the Lord shall be revealed
>   As He purifies our lives:
> And the whole wide world shall see the bride prepared
>   As the darkness comes to the light.
>
> We'll make a highway for the Lord,
>   We'll make a highway for King Jesus,
> We'll make a highway for the Bridegroom to return.[1]

> PRAYER [MB]: *O God, we pray that Thy glory shall come down upon us; that there shall be a burning up of sin,*

*that Thy glory may come down upon the altar of
sacrifice, that deep, inward, real sacrifice of self shall
be made, so that Thy glory may be able to rest upon
us. O Father, we are shutting Thee out by the stench of
our sin, and we long for Thy glory to be revealed, and
for self to be crucified so that the glory of the Lord
shall have a resting place and no sin bar Him or turn
Him away. O come down, Thou glorious One; let Thy
glory reach down from the very Heaven into the place
where we are. Glorify Thy Son in our hearts and
minds.*

Notes

1   From "Prepare the way for Jesus to return", by Pip
    and Alison Roseblade (© Restoration Music,
    1983).

APPENDIX II

Calvinism vs Arminianism

The controversy between Arminianism and Calvinism is usefully summarized in a booklet by W.J. Seaton, entitled *The Five Points of Calvinism*.[1] He writes:

> The Five Points of Arminianism were, broadly speaking, as follows:
>
> 1. *Free will, or human ability.* This taught that man, although affected by the Fall, was not totally incapable of choosing spiritual good, and was able to exercise faith in God in order to receive the gospel and thus bring himself into possession of salvation.
>
> 2. *Conditional election.* This taught that God laid His hands upon those individuals who, He knew — or foresaw — would respond to the gospel. God elected those that He saw would want to be saved of their own free will...
>
> 3. *Universal redemption, or general atonement.* This taught that Christ died to save all men; but only in a *potential* fashion. Christ's death enabled God to pardon sinners, but only on condition that they believed.
>
> 4. *The work of the Holy Spirit in regeneration limited by the human will.* This taught that the Holy Spirit, as He began to work to bring a person to Christ, could be effectually resisted and His purposes frustrated. He could not impart life unless the sinner was willing to have this life imparted.
>
> 5. *Falling from grace.* This taught that a saved man could fall finally from salvation....

The Five Points of Calvinism formulated by the Synod

of Dort in 1618 to counter the Arminian system may be presented as an acrostic on the word TULIP:

T   Total Depravity (i.e. Total Inability)
U   Unconditional Election
L   Limited Atonement (i.e. Particular Redemption)
I   Irresistible Calling
P   Perseverance of the Saints

Seaton, a supporter of Calvinism, comments:

As can be readily seen, these set themselves in complete opposition to the Five Points of Arminianism. Man is totally unable to save himself on account of the Fall in the Garden of Eden being a *total* fall. If unable to save himself, then God must save. If God must save, then God must be free to save whom He will. If God has decreed to save whom He will, then it is for those that Christ made atonement on the Cross. If Christ died for them, then the Holy Spirit will effectually call them into that salvation. If salvation then from the beginning has been of God, the end will also be of God and the saints will persevere to eternal joy.

Note

1   The Banner of Truth Trust, 1970. I am grateful to the Rev Alasdair Gollan for giving me a copy of this booklet. Extracts are taken from pp. 7–8.

NOTE TO READERS

If you would like to enquire further about issues raised in this book or if you feel that the author could be of help, you are invited to write to him at 27 Denholm Street, Greenock, PA16 8RH, Scotland, or telephone 0475 87432.

It may also be of interest to know that the author is normally involved in five conferences in Scotland each year — New Year, Easter, July, August and October. Friends gather from many parts of Britain. An open invitation is extended to all and particularly to those interested in the Baptism in the Holy Spirit and related themes. Details will be provided on enquiry.

BY THE SAME AUTHOR

Reflections on the Baptism in the Holy Spirit *£2.25* This book is already proving very popular and is being used in bringing people into the baptism in the Spirit. It has been described as one of the clearest, most incisive books on this subject.

Reflections on the Gifts of the Spirit *£2.75* Deals in an original way with its subject. The chapters on miracles, healings and discernment (with exorcism) have roused great interest and led to positive action. Anecdotes and illustrations have been much appreciated.

Reflections on a Song of Love *£1.25* A highly original commentary on 1 Cor 13. The drawing power of love pervades this fascinating study. The author shows very clearly how this chapter fully supports and in no way detracts from the doctrine of Pentecost.

A Trumpet Call to Women *£2.50* Presents a strong case from Scripture for greater involvement of women in ministry. It throws much light on those portions which on the surface seem to put women in a subject role. It includes the testimony of Elizabeth H. Taylor, a lady much used of God. A stirring book, demanding a response — a call to action.

Consider Him *£2.25* Considers a number of the qualities of Christ. He Himself seems to speak from the pages of the book, both in the main text and in the testimony of

Jennifer Jack, whose selfless presentation truly leaves the reader to consider Christ.

Battle for the Body *£2.95* It will take courage to face the truths highlighted in this original approach to fundamental issues of sanctification. The second part presents the powerful testimony of John Hamilton — a preacher widely known and loved.

The Clash of Tongues: With Glimpses of Revival *£2.75* Part One is a commentary on 1 Cor 14. It deals in detail with some of the more difficult questions. Part Two deals with the relationship between revival and Pentecost and refers to the 1939 and 1949 revivals in Lewis, introducing a number of people who were involved in the first of these — particularly Mary MacLean, whose remarkable testimony is related. This book may particularly appeal to people studiously inclined.

The Incomparable Christ *£2.75* Part One deals with the gospel. It faces honestly the questions of Christ's resurrection and that of all men. It deals in a direct way with the doctrine of hell and eternal judgment, and gives practical instruction on the way of salvation. Part Two presents the remarkable testimonies of two young ladies.

Gospel Vignettes *£2.95* Focuses attention on various facets of the gospel, with chapter titles like: Ye Must Be Born Again, The Life-Giving Water, Weighed in the Balances, Behold I Stand at the Door and Knock, The Hour of Decision. Includes testimonies of three people whose lives have been transformed by Christ, to one of whom Christ Himself appeared. Useful in the gospel, but introducing the Pentecostal dimension.

Reflections from Abraham *£2.50* Outlines spiritual principles seen in the life of Abraham. It deals with his call and ours, the mountain as distinct from the valley life, intercession, Lot in Sodom, the sacrifice of Isaac and the way of faith. Part Two tells of the action of God in the life of Dorothy Jennings, to whom Abraham has been of particular significance.

Reflections from Moses: With the Testimony of Dan McVicar *£2.99* Part One shows the outworking of spiritual principles such as the calling and training of a man of God, the need to start from holy ground, deliverance from bondage, and the consequences of Moses' failure in a critical hour. Part Two presents the well-known evangelist Dan McVicar's story in his own words. The conversion of this militant communist and the intervention of God in the lives of his parents make thrilling reading.

Christ the Deliverer *£2.99* Deals with both physical and spiritual deliverance. It includes a number of remarkable testimonies to healing, e.g. from blindness, manic depression, ME, rheumatoid arthritis, spinal injury, phobias, nightmares. It speaks of the appearance of angels, touches on revival and analyses the theory of 'visualization'.

Christian Fundamentals *£3.50* Part One deals with the individual and his needs in the realms of Salvation, Baptism in the Spirit, and Deliverance. Part Two focuses on the outflow of the life of God to meet the needs of others through Vocal, Hidden and Open Power Ministries. The End Times are the subject of Part Three. The testimony of Mary Black is included in this powerfully written book.

Reflections from David *£3.75* This searching book shows a man after God's own heart in the glory of his achievements and the tragedy of his failings. Divine retribution and forgiveness, the joy of deliverance, and the action of God in present-day lives are all examined.

Pioneers of the Spiritual Way *£4.99* From a lost Eden our race walked a lost road, occasionally experiencing higher things as pioneers of the spiritual way led upwards. The impassable barrier between God and man was finally removed as the last Adam blasted a way through: Christ, bringing many sons to glory.

Revival: Personal Encounters *£3.99* From the treasure chest of memory the author brings a series of revival-related incidents. We hear of Studd, Burton and Salter and of revival in the Congo and Rwanda. More is revealed of the moving of God in Lewis and at an unusual Scottish school camp. A contemporary scene in Brazil brings revival very close. The highly original testimony of Alison Speirs brings the fact and challenge right to our doorstep.

Revival: Living in the Realities For a revived or a revival-conscious people a high level of Christian living is immediately presented. The experience of revival has to be outlived. This book ponders issues such as spiritual warfare, what it means to be imitators of Christ, the need to progress from forgiveness to love for those who do us harm, and the mystery of the love of God itself. Moving stories of healing are included. An unusual and thought-provoking approach.

BOOK ORDERS

The books advertised on the previous pages are being made available to Christian booksellers throughout the country, but if you have any difficulty in obtaining your supply, you may order directly from New Dawn Books, c/o 27 Denholm Street, Greenock, Scotland, PA16 8RH.

·············· **ORDER FORM** ··············

Please send me the books indicated below:

Quantity	Title	Price
	Reflections on the Baptism in the Holy Spirit	£2.25
	Reflections on the Gifts of the Spirit	£2.75
	Reflections on a Song of Love (A commentary on 1 Cor 13)	£1.25
	A Trumpet Call to Women	£2.50
	Consider Him (Twelve Qualities of Christ)	£2.25
	Battle for the Body	£2.95
	The Clash of Tongues: With Glimpses of Revival	£2.75
	The Incomparable Christ	£2.75
	Gospel Vignettes	£2.95
	Reflections from Abraham	£2.50
	Reflections from Moses: With the testimony of Dan McVicar	£2.99
	Christ the Deliverer	£2.99
	Christian Fundamentals	£3.50
	Reflections from David	£3.50
	Pioneers of the Spiritual Way	£4.99
	Revival: Including the Prophetic Vision of Jean Darnall	£3.99
	Revival: Personal Encounters	£4.50
	Revival: Living in the Realities	£

Signature ....

Address ....

....

....

When ordering please send purchase price plus 40p per book to help cover the cost of postage and packaging.

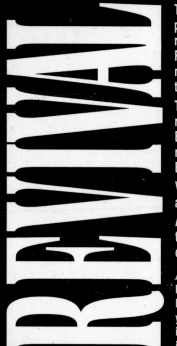

This book directs readers to the past in order to prepare for coming days. Patterns and principles of revival are reviewed in connection with Charles G. Finney in America, the Methodist awakening and, nearer our own times, the Welsh revival of 1904 and the Lewis revival of 1949.

There is a strong emphasis on the near future with reference to the now famous vision of Jean Darnall. Breaking out in the north of Scotland, the coming revival is envisaged as moving swiftly south, into England and across the Channel.

Very remarkable and unusual features of this event are given in close detail.

A sermon of Jean Darnall's is incorporated in the text. This is a book to teach, encourage and deeply challenge readers.

About the Author

Formerly a head teacher of secondary schools, Hugh Black is a leader of the Struthers Memorial group of churches. For many years he has been used in evangelism and in bringing people into the baptism in the Spirit. In recent years he has seen an increasing number of healings and deliverances.

NEW DAWN BOOKS

ISBN 1-870944-15-1

Price £3.99

9 781870 944151 >